Why Are We Losing the Kids?

Why Are We Losing the Kids?

Sandra M. Platt

ISBN-13: 978-1539596202
ISBN-10: 1539596206

DEDICATION

To David, Erin, Cole and Sam. I'm so proud and thankful to be your Mom.

CONTENTS

ACKNOWLEDGMENTS

I would like to acknowledge with utmost gratitude, my husband Jim, who has been an unwavering support for all my projects and Kim, my dear friend and soul-winning partner who always encourages me to stand for truth.

CHAPTER 1
WHY ARE WE LOSING THE KIDS?

As Christian women, there is nothing more heart breaking than to see our children and grandchildren turn from God. We want so much to see them saved, that we spend thousands of dollars, and sacrifice countless hours to VBS, Bible clubs, Youth groups, Church camp, and children's parties every year. We work until we drop trying to bring children in through our programs in hopes of winning them to Christ. Many wonderfully godly people commit their entire lives to children's ministries, only to see these children turn from God. With our extensive efforts, why are we still losing them?

I personally have heard many answers to this question ranging from music and entertainment, to hypocrisy in the leadership, to not enough of a Church family bond. While these issues surely play a part, they fail to identify the true problem. These suggestions may help us to make Church more appealing for them and help us to be better examples, but these are only band-aid fixes for the deeper problem.

When I moved to central Pennsylvania in 2003, I was thrilled to see such a large community of Christians. It was such a change from living in the New Haven area of CT. where there were very few Bible believing Churches. Soon however, I began to see that every door we knocked on was answered by a professing Christian.

It seemed that practically everyone in town professed to have been saved as a child. Evidences to support these claims however, was conspicuously absent.

These converts were the fruits of a local Church's children's ministries. They were brought in for fun and games, many just for one night, led through a prayer and sent home with an assurance of salvation. If simply getting someone to repeat a prayer was biblical salvation, I would have to commend these diligent efforts; but it isn't.

Now these grown-up children walk and talk and act like the world, live in the world, even loving the world, and though they do not appear to love God, they believe that they are saved. Many of these have never attended Church regularly, and even their own children who once did, no longer do.

Why are the kids really leaving the Church?

If we will look to the holy scriptures, it's really not that difficult to find the answer. I know it is not the answer we want; but if we are ever going to change things, we must face the truth.

"They went out from us, but they were not of us; for if they had been of us, they would no doubt have continued with us: but they went out, that they might be made manifest that they were not all of us" (1 John 2:19).

If at the first opportunity to step out from under parental authority, and to be answerable for themselves, young people choose to walk away from God, it's clear that their hearts are not toward God. Why do they go off and live like the unsaved? Why is it so hard for us to see that it's because they are unsaved?

"Ye shall know them by their fruits. Do men gather grapes of thorns, or figs of thistles? Even so every good tree bringeth forth good fruit; but a corrupt tree bringeth forth evil fruit. A good tree cannot bring forth evil fruit, neither can a corrupt tree bring forth good fruit. Every tree that bringeth not forth good fruit is hewn down, and cast into the fire. Wherefore by their fruits ye shall know them (Matthew 7:16-20).

How many scriptures do we have to ignore to convince ourselves that we are getting all these kids saved just because we led them through prayers? The vast majority of children that we lead to the Lord turn away from God, and go out into the world embracing every sin imaginable never to darken the doors of a Church again; and we tell ourselves that at least they got saved when they were three or five, or whatever age, so that we can sleep at night.

According to the Bible and even to our own consciences, we know that's probably far from true. No matter what excuses we might make to others for our false converts, we cannot hide the truth from God.

We need to seriously ask ourselves why we are so anxious to insist that our converts really are saved, despite an abundance of evidence to the contrary. Can we honestly say that it is for their benefit?

We may think it is a small thing if a child makes a false profession, or that it might help them to choose right later; but we may in fact be doing more damage than good.

Can a four-year-old get saved?

The aim of most children's ministries is to convince children to *accept Jesus* or *ask him into their hearts* at the earliest possible age. Sadly, this is often before they even know what sin is, let alone repentance toward God. Who would ever expect a toddler to understand the concepts of repentance and faith? Grownups struggle with understanding these things, and yet we begin pressuring these children for a *decision* right out of the nursery.

We fear to scare them with talk about Hell; and yet we think they should be accountable to God for their sin and press them to take responsibility for their own souls. Then, we trust that these toddlers and preschoolers who do not know their right hands from their lefts, really meant that decision we coerced them into making. What are we thinking? How did salvation become such a small thing to us that we view it as merely coercing a prayer from a child?

I recently heard testimony and praise about a four year-old child that *got saved*. The tearful story of the ecstatic Grandmother of the child evoked an emotional celebration within our local congregation. "Halleluiahs" and "Praise the Lords" were heard from some, as others smiled and nodded their approval. I honestly had to wonder, "Am I really the only one who thinks this is a bit unlikely?"

You might ask, "Don't you believe that a four year- old can be saved?" Well, if you mean by that: "Can a four-year-old be taught a couple of Bible verses and catch phrases and told to love Jesus (the unseen person he has never met), and then led to repeat a prayer with the promise of Heaven as a reward?" Absolutely! Without a doubt! I do believe that he can perform this act. This however, IS NOT biblical salvation. Do people honestly believe that it is?

Now, on the other hand, if you were to ask whether I believe that a four year- old can understand his lost condition as a sinner condemned before a righteous God to an eternity in Hell, repent and trust in Jesus Christ alone as his only hope of forgiveness; I would have to say that I think it is doubtful. Granted, with God, all things are possible. There may possibly be children that young who do indeed have great spiritual understanding beyond their years, but as much as every Mother wants to believe that their child is such a spiritual phenomenon; I would imagine that it is truly rare.

Almost every child in Church today believes in Jesus. "... the devils also believe, and tremble" (James 2:19).

Simply believing in the existence of Jesus or the facts of his death, burial and resurrection is NOT salvation. That does not mean that they are saved. Praying a prayer is also NOT salvation. Most of these children also believe in Santa. That does not make them elves, or even very discerning. I'm pretty sure we would be equally successful in coercing a prayer to Santa or to the Easter Bunny.

I have heard many give their own testimonies of *getting saved* at a tender age such as this. Often, they have fond memories of kneeling before a manger scene or making a decision somewhere, but rarely is repentance toward God or even genuine faith in Christ even expressed.

Most often, praying a prayer is the highlight of their memory, with no testimony of changed life. Many even confess that they lived apart from God for a great deal of time after their conversion and experienced a *recommitment* later in their lives, in which sanctification and a changed life began.

Those things should begin *with* salvation, not years after. Can I suggest to you that if we were to examine these accounts biblically, we would have to conclude that salvation was probably the thing that came later, and not just a recommitment? Do we honestly believe that the Holy Spirit of our holy and perfect God could suddenly begin to dwell within the body of even the smallest human being and not witness of itself or show forth evidences?

Some may argue that children just don't have much sin to change from, especially children who grow up in Church. Therefore, they reason, a change would not be evident, seeing these were good kids to start with Well, according to the Bible, if they were not sinners saved by grace then they are NOT SAVED at all.

"When Jesus heard it, he saith unto them, They that are whole have no need of the physician, but they that are sick: I came not to call the righteous, but sinners to repentance" (Mark 2:17).

Without a correct understanding of what sin is, and a genuine repentance toward God, true saving faith in Christ is not even possible. Yet we tell these children sometimes at three and four years old, to *just accept Jesus.*

They say the prayer we tell them to say, learn how to *act* like Christians, play the games, eat the candy and yet most often, they are not regenerated. They do not become new creatures, and nothing really changes in their hearts.

They try the false salvation we offer according to our Easy Believeism gospel, but if they are not born again, to them, this false salvation represents falseness on every level of Christianity. Instead of strengthening them in the word and preparing them to receive the Savior, we are inoculating them against the gospel. That is why we are losing the kids.

When they finally do know good from evil and desire to make a decision of their own, often the only decision left to make is to reject this Christianity that has never been real to them anyway. When they are old enough to choose for themselves, is it really a wonder that they leave at the first opportunity and end the charade?

Whether you're a Mom or a teacher, it's time to take responsibility for what we're teaching and guard our kids against such harmful practices.

Simply asking Jesus into your heart is not the biblical gospel we have been called to preach. *This* **is Easy Believeism.**

Somehow, we have gotten so caught up in our games and snacks and tallying up our numbers, that we haven't even noticed that we have embraced "another gospel".

I know this is difficult to even consider, but we must. If we are consistently creating false converts (corrupt fruit), we MUST examine the seed we are sowing.

> "I marvel that ye are so soon removed from him that called you into the grace of Christ unto another gospel: Which is not another; but there be some that trouble you, and would pervert the gospel of Christ. But though we, or an angel from heaven, preach any other gospel unto you than that which we have preached unto you, let him be accursed. As we said before, so say I now again, If any man preach any other gospel unto you than that ye have received, let him be accursed" (Galatians 1:6-9).

"Let him be accursed…" That ought to be a sobering thought. Paul wasn't messing around. Bringing another gospel was no secondary infraction. It was a major concern and one that was seriously condemned by Paul, under the inspiration of the Holy Spirit. That is how serious the preaching of the gospel is. The gospel of Jesus Christ is the foundation of our very belief system. Any who would distort it, or take away from its message are not to be tolerated patiently, but accursed. We cannot take this lightly.

> "I marvel that ye are so soon removed from him that called you into the grace of Christ unto another gospel: Which is not another; but there be some that trouble you, and would pervert the gospel of Christ" (Galatians 1:6-7).

Paul warns against anything that would pervert or distort the gospel message. He could not believe that they would be so easily led astray from the gospel which he had preached unto them. What about us? Have we believed another gospel?

To many within Fundamental, Bible-believing Churches, this question might sound absurd. Many such Churches today pride themselves on their strict stand on Bible doctrine and would find it difficult to even consider that they have been deceived by a false gospel, but something this serious deserves our most earnest consideration.

No matter how sincere we may be, if the gospel we are preaching is not the true gospel message, and we are not truly leading others to the Lord, then everything we are doing is for nothing. And what's worse, we are not just fruitless but according to the scriptures, accursed!

> "Every man's work shall be made manifest: for the day shall declare it, because it shall be revealed by fire; and the fire shall try every man's work of what sort it is" (1 Corinthians 3:13).

Not only will our works be tried by fire and burn up as wood, hay and stubble, but also our converts. If they are not genuinely saved, they too will be burned with the fires of Hell. We may be willing to risk our own rewards, but are we willing to risk the souls of these children as well as adults that may be believing "another gospel"?

Many confronted with the truth of this false doctrine, willfully refuse to change. A woman I once knew told me that if these things were truly so, then it would mean that the majority of her converts were probably false and her efforts over the years in vain, and she simply would not accept that. To her credit, she did spend some time praying and searching her heart.

Sadly, she decided that the failure was not in her, *or* in her methods. She continues to do that which is right in her own eyes, preaching and teaching a false gospel message of *simply ask Jesus into your heart* to those who often do not even know what sin is, then offering assurances based upon their professions. Will we also allow our pride to rule us that way? Is our pride worth sending so many to Hell with a false gospel?

I would beg you to please, as far as you are able, put aside anything that might cloud your reason, -your emotions, experiences, relationships and all the things you have been taught by men, and honestly examine your own gospel message, diligently comparing it with the scriptures. I believe that if you will prayerfully do this, you will very easily see how far we've strayed. What we are doing and teaching today is not the biblical gospel.

CHAPTER 2
WHAT IS THE BIBLCAL MESSAGE WE ARE CALLED TO PREACH?

"And he said unto them, Go ye into all the world, and preach the gospel to every creature" (Mark 16:15).

What is the gospel? Most well-Churched Christians, when asked this question, would immediately reference 1Corinthians 15:1-4.

"Moreover, brethren, I declare unto you the gospel which I preached unto you, which also ye have received, and wherein ye stand; By which also ye are saved, if ye keep in memory what I preached unto you, unless ye have believed in vain. For I delivered unto you first of all that which I also received, how that Christ died for our sins according to the scriptures; And that he was buried, and that he rose again the third day according to the scriptures" (1 Corinthians 15:1-4).

Of course, we know that this *is* the gospel- the good news of what our precious Savior Jesus Christ has done on behalf of sinful man. The death, burial and resurrection of Christ is the gospel in a nutshell. But, is this the *whole* message we are called to preach and teach?

Many today insist that since Paul did not mention repentance in this section of scripture, that repentance is not part of the message we are called to preach. They reason that since the Apostle Paul summarized the gospel as Jesus' death burial and resurrection in this portion of scripture, (without mentioning repentance) that simply preaching these facts with an admonition to *ask Jesus into your heart* is a sufficient message for evangelism.

Can we honestly say that "…how that Christ died for our sins according to the scriptures; And that he was buried, and that he rose again the third day according to the scriptures…"(1Corinithians 15:3-4) is the *complete* message we are called to preach to the ends of the earth?

"And that **repentance and remission of sins** should be preached in his name **among all nations, beginning at Jerusalem**" (Luke 24:47 emphasis mine).

Repentance was clearly part of the great commission.

Scripture shows that Paul *did* indeed preach repentance.

"But shewed first unto them of Damascus, and at Jerusalem, and throughout all the coasts of Judaea, and then to the Gentiles, that they should repent and turn to God, and do works meet for repentance" (Acts 26:20).

"And the times of this ignorance God winked at; but now commandeth all men every where to repent" (Acts 17:30).

So, did something change prior to the writing of this passage that prompted Paul to leave out repentance? Certainly, not!

Why did Paul *not* mention repentance when he speaks of the gospel in 1 Corinthians 15?

In reading 1Corinthians in its proper context, 2 points shed light on this question:
1.The Audience
Paul's letter to the Corinthians is obviously, a letter to a Church, which means that he is speaking to believers. When preaching to those who claim to be believers, or Brethren, the message is often quite different than a message for unbelievers or those whom you are seeking to evangelize.

e.g.: "I wrote unto you in an epistle not to company with fornicators: Yet not altogether with the fornicators of this world, or with the covetous, or extortioners, or with idolaters; for then must ye needs go out of the world. But now I have written unto you not to keep company, if any man that is called a brother be a fornicator, or covetous, or an idolater, or a railer, or a drunkard, or an extortioner; with such an one no not to eat. For what have I to do to judge them also that are without? do not ye judge them that are within? But them that are without God judgeth. Therefore put away from among yourselves that wicked person" (1Corinthians 5:9-13).

Here we see that Paul's instructions for believers were very different than the instructions he would have for unbelievers. Quite simply, the reason Paul's letters to the Churches did not specifically address repentance regarding salvation could be that he was addressing those who were already saved and had already come to repentance. We do not see specific instructions for Evangelism or sermons to the unsaved recorded within these letters because they were written *to* the Churches (believers). However, when we look at the book of Acts, which does tell us in detail what Paul preached, we see that Paul's message to the unsaved was clearly a message of repentance and faith.

"Testifying both to the Jews, and also to the Greeks, repentance toward God, and faith toward our Lord Jesus Christ" (Acts 20:21).

"Which when the apostles, Barnabas and Paul, heard of, they rent their clothes, and ran in among the people, crying out, And saying, Sirs, why do ye these things? We also are men of like passions with you, and preach unto you that ye should turn from these vanities unto the living God, which made heaven, and earth, and the sea, and all things that are therein" (Acts 14:14-15).

"And the times of this ignorance God winked at; but now commandeth all men every where to repent" (Acts 17:30).

While that may seem to oversimplify the issue, I believe the next point answers the question a bit more clearly.

2. The Purpose.
1 Corinthians was written by Paul to address various issues that had arisen within the Church. He spends the first 14 chapters addressing sin and error and establishing doctrine regarding questions raised, e.g.: division, carnality, fornication, going to law against one another, marital issues, the eating of meats offered to idols, liberties, and a rather large section on correcting misunderstanding regarding spiritual gifts, ending in chapter 14.

In chapter 15, he lays the groundwork to address yet another error that had begun to trouble the Church- the question of the resurrection of the dead. He sets forth the message of Christ's death, burial and resurrection, reminding them how that he has already taught them this, pointing out the eyewitnesses which testified to these. Then he goes on to ask:

"Now if Christ be preached that he rose from the dead, how say some among you that there is no resurrection of the dead? But if there be no resurrection of the dead, then is Christ not risen" (1 Corinthians 15:12-13).

He explains to them that without Christ's resurrection, his preaching would be in vain, and our faith would be pointless, for we would be without hope. When he describes the gospel in this passage, it is not *to unbelievers* for the purpose of evangelization, but to believers for the purpose of proving Christ's resurrection.

"For I delivered unto you first of all that which I also received, how that Christ died for our sins according to the scriptures; And that he was buried, and that he rose again the third day according to the scriptures: And that he was seen of Cephas, then of the twelve: After that, he was seen of above five hundred brethren at once; of whom the greater part remain unto this present, but some are fallen asleep. After that, he was seen of James; then of all the apostles. And last of all he was seen of me also, as of one born out of due time" (1 Corinthians 15:3-8).

Paul's focus is on showing Christ's resurrection and why it is essential to believe it. His intent is to correct and instruct believers, it was not to evangelize the lost or to teach evangelism. He then goes on to teach of the rapture and deliverance of those who died already (which hinge upon the resurrection).

He finishes the letter with chapter 16 which discusses the collection for the saints and his closing thoughts. These are just 2 likely reasons Paul did not specifically mention repentance within this passage.

Paul's message did not change, dropping repentance as some would suggest.

The Gospel message preached by Paul and the apostles, to Jew and Gentile alike, has always been Repentance toward God and Faith Toward Jesus Christ.

"And how I kept back nothing that was profitable unto you, but have shewed you, and have taught you publickly, and from house to house, Testifying both to the Jews, and also to the Greeks, repentance toward God, and faith toward our Lord Jesus Christ" (Acts 20:20-21).

Paul tells us that he did not keep anything back. He gave them the *whole* counsel of God- "repentance toward God and faith toward our Lord and Savior Jesus Christ" (Acts 20:21). Paul's message always included repentance, as did the message of the other Apostles.

In the book of Acts, we read of Paul reasoning and disputing in the synagogue for days at a time. In chapter 17 we see him preaching to the men of Athens. He did not simply give an ABC's or 123's gospel message; he preached to them the identity of God, who he is, his hand in creation & his personal relationship and availability to men. He preached God's righteous judgment and the coming resurrection as well as the good news of Jesus Christ. Then when some said they would hear him again, and clung to him, he continued preaching to them. As a matter of fact, NEVER did he lead anyone through a prayer or pronounce them saved, even if they *were* convicted. Instead, he simply instructed those who repented and believed to be baptized.

When Peter preached on the day of Pentecost, "they were pricked in their heart, and said unto Peter and to the rest of the apostles, Men and brethren, what shall we do?" (Acts 2:37).

Why? Because Peter preached to them about their sin against God first, how that they had rejected and crucified their long-awaited Savior that died to bring salvation to them.

"Therefore let all the house of Israel know assuredly, that God hath made that same Jesus, whom ye have crucified, both Lord and Christ" (Acts 2:36).

In the horror of their realization they asked, "what shall we do?" (to take away their sins and be made right with God). Peter's answer certainly was not, "Repeat this prayer after me." No, Peter told them to repent and be baptized.

"Then Peter said unto them, Repent, and be baptized every one of you in the name of Jesus Christ for the remission of sins, and ye shall receive the gift of the Holy Ghost" (Acts 2:38).

We read in Acts 7:54 that when Stephen preached, his hearers were so angered that they gnashed upon him with their teeth and finally stoned him to death. Was this because he preached a positive message of "Hey, do you want to know how you can go to Heaven when you die? Just say this simple prayer." No. (I would suggest that if he had said something like that, he would have lived considerably longer than he did.) He too, told them of their sin and condemnation before God. The true biblical Gospel always included repentance toward God.

Some point to other passages which also do not mention repentance. This lack of mention does not negate scriptures such as these we have already looked at, which do clearly spell out the necessity of repentance in salvation. There are also many passages which mention repentance only and do not mention faith. We would never dare suggest that repentance without faith saves.

"But go ye and learn what that meaneth, I will have mercy, and not sacrifice: for I am not come to call the righteous, but sinners to repentance" (Matthew 9:13).

"I say unto you, that likewise joy shall be in heaven over one sinner that repenteth, more than over ninety and nine just persons, which need no repentance" (Luke 15:7).

"The Lord is not slack concerning his promise, as some men count slackness; but is longsuffering to us-ward, not willing that any should perish, but that all should come to repentance" (2 Peter 3:9).

"When they heard these things, they held their peace, and glorified God, saying, Then hath God also to the Gentiles granted repentance unto life" (Acts 11:18).

The good news of the gospel is not only that Christ died and rose again the third day to save us from our sins. The good news is that our creator, a thrice holy God would love sinful man enough to desire a relationship with him, and that he wants so much to bridge the separation caused by our sin that he was willing to sacrifice his only son to reconcile us to himself.

Be ye reconciled to God

"For God so loved the world, that he gave his only begotten Son, that whosoever believeth in him should not perish, but have everlasting life" (John 3:16).

What is the message that we should be proclaiming?

"To wit, that God was in Christ, reconciling the world unto himself, not imputing their trespasses unto them; **and hath committed unto us the word of reconciliation.** Now then we are ambassadors for Christ, as though God did beseech you by us: we pray you in Christ's stead, **be ye reconciled to God**" (2 Corinthians 5:19-20 emphasis mine).

Jesus Christ came to do the will of the Father, which was to reconcile fallen man to himself.

"Then said Jesus to them again, Peace be unto you: as my Father hath sent me, even so send I you" (John 20:21).

The message committed to us is the message of reconciliation.

"And that every tongue should confess that Jesus Christ is Lord, **to the glory of God the Father**" (Philippians 2:11 emphasis mine).

The message originally preached by the apostles is a message of reconciliation to God through faith in Jesus Christ. Why? Because in our natural state, we are all separated from God. What is it that separates us from God? Sin. In its simplest form, it is an unwillingness to obey his laws, a rebellion against God. Without repentance from sin, there can be no reconciliation and of course, no salvation.

"...for sin is the transgression of the law" (1 John 3:4).

Repentance is an undeniable concept illustrated throughout the Bible.

The Old Testament is filled with stories of repentance toward God. God desires so much to give to man what he does not deserve, mercy, blessings and new life. The children of Israel are a picture to us, showing Gods message to mankind- that if they would obey him and trust him then they would have blessing and health, but if they rebelled and turned away from serving him, they would have punishment, wrath, illness, and ultimately destruction.

"A blessing, if ye obey the commandments of the LORD your God, which I command you this day: And a curse, if ye will not obey the commandments of the LORD your God, but turn aside out of the way which I command you this day, to go after other gods, which ye have not known" (Deuteronomy 11:27-28).

"Ye shall walk after the LORD your God, and fear him, and keep his commandments, and obey his voice, and ye shall serve him, and cleave unto him" (Deuteronomy 13:4).

Despite his goodness, over and over we see that foolish Israel would not cleave unto him, but allowed their sins to separate them from him. When God's judgment and wrath came upon them, they would sorrowfully repent and turn to him once again. In their rebellion, they could not enjoy God's blessings, but when they repented, (turned from their rebellion and became willing once again to be reconciled to God) He restored to them the blessings and peace they could not receive in their disobedience.

"Your iniquities have turned away these things, and your sins have withholden good things from you" (Jeremiah 5:25).

"... Wherefore he saith, God resisteth the proud, but giveth grace unto the humble" (James 4:6).

"The LORD is nigh unto them that are of a broken heart; and saveth such as be of a contrite spirit" (Psalms 34:18).

"Salvation is far from the wicked: for they seek not thy statutes" (Psalms 119:155).

Repentance is not a difficult or confusing word. What makes it difficult is reconciling today's methods with the traditional, biblical understanding of repentance. This is what leads to the confusion. Anytime, we demand that the normal, logical interpretation of a word be set aside, we can be sure the Devil is behind it. Repentance is a distaste for and *willingness* to turn from sin and be reconciled to God. Any gospel message that does not include repentance is a false gospel. I'm thankful to be in a Church that still preaches repentance, but we must be sure that we are also carrying this over into our children's ministries and soul-winning efforts.

What is the biblical definition of repentance?

The biblical definition of repentance according to Strong's Greek Lexicon: The KJV translates Strong's G3341 in the following manner: repentance. μετάνοια metánoia, met-an'-oy-ah; from G3340; (subjectively) compunction (for guilt, including reformation); by implication, reversal (of (another's) decision):—repentance. to change one's mind, i.e. to repent to change one's mind for better, heartily to amend with abhorrence of one's past sins.

'Repentance (metanoia, 'change of mind') involves a turning with contrition from sin to God; the repentant sinner is in the proper condition to accept the divine forgiveness.' (F. F. Bruce. The Acts of the Apostles [Greek Text Commentary], London: Tyndale, 1952, p. 97.) ("G3341 - metanoia - Strong's Greek Lexicon (KJV)." Blue Letter Bible. Accessed 1 Mar, 2017.)

Repentance is a change of mind which results in a change of actions. Repentance includes a realization and sorrow for sin, resulting from conviction of the Holy Spirit.

"And when he is come, he will reprove the world of sin, and of righteousness, and of judgment" (John 16:8).

Once we see ourselves the way God does, and the vileness of our sin, we no longer embrace it and cherish it, but are repulsed by it. Repentance is NOT a complete abandonment of sin or reformation, but a sorrow and distaste for the things that displease God, and a desire to turn from it which brings about evidences or fruits of repentance.

"Bring forth therefore fruits meet for repentance" (Matthew 3:8).

Unbelief to belief?

Today many have attempted to change the definition of repentance to mean that repentance is merely a change of mind from unbelief (in Christ) to belief (in Christ) with no connection to sin whatsoever. Therefore, they reason, it is not necessary to preach repentance from sin, but only belief in Christ. John 3:18 is claimed as support for their argument.

> "He that believeth on him is not condemned: but he that believeth not is condemned already, because he hath not believed in the name of the only begotten Son of God" (John 3:18).

According to this verse, they reason that the only sin that will truly condemn a man to Hell is the sin of unbelief in Christ, and therefore the only sin that needs to be repented of. Repentance, according to this thinking is merely a change of mind from unbelief to belief.

Looking at this verse alone, seems to support that idea quite nicely, however comparing scripture with scripture we see that is not true. It was not the sin of unbelief in Christ that Adam committed which brought sin and death upon us all. It was disobedience.

> "For as by one man's disobedience many were made sinners, so by the obedience of one shall many be made righteous" (Romans 5:19).

Because of sin, we are all *already* condemned. Unbelief in Jesus Christ, the Savior God has provided, seals our fate as condemned sinners and prevents our salvation, but it is sin that brought God's wrath in the first place and it is sin that we must repent of.

Sadly, this error of preaching repentance as turning from unbelief in Christ to belief, originally introduced by super salesmen soul-winners, has been adopted by multitudes of preachers and teachers throughout Protestant Christianity. The reasons for this I'm sure, are obvious. The truth that man must repent of his sin and turn to God, trusting in his son, Jesus Christ to save him from his sins is difficult for most to swallow. Preaching belief in Christ alone, without repentance from sin, would certainly make the gospel more palatable. If all man had to repent of was his unbelief in Christ, the message would be an easy one to hear.

Believing in the facts of the gospel and even of who Christ is, are not difficult. This was also not the message of Christ himself. When the rich young ruler, came to him, asking what he must do to be saved, Jesus did not say, "Simply believe in me." This ruler must have known who Jesus was and trusted that he could give him the words of life to be saved. Jesus could have easily led him to make a profession of faith.

"And Jesus said unto him, Why callest thou me good? none is good, save one, that is, God. Thou knowest the commandments, Do not commit adultery, Do not kill, Do not steal, Do not bear false witness, Honour thy father and thy mother. And he said, All these have I kept from my youth up" (Luke 18:19-21).

Instead of merely telling him to pray a prayer and believe in him, Jesus, knowing his heart, showed him how sinful he truly was.

"Now when Jesus heard these things, he said unto him, Yet lackest thou one thing: sell all that thou hast, and distribute unto the poor, and thou shalt have treasure in heaven: and come, follow me. And when he heard this, he was very sorrowful: for he was very rich" (Luke 18:22-23).

Christ was calling him to love God above all else (including his riches) and to love his neighbor as himself (sacrificially giving to him). This was an act of repentance toward God Christ was calling him to, a change of mind leading to a change of action. If repentance was merely turning from unbelief (in Christ) to belief, then why would this man go away sorrowful and unsaved?

We see a similar incident in Acts 24:24-25. Felix sent for Paul to come and speak to him, for the specific reason of hearing about faith in Jesus Christ. However, when Paul spoke, he did not merely speak of Christ's death, burial and resurrection and admonish Felix to only believe. He spoke to him of righteousness and the judgment to come, so that Felix would understand his need to repent and trust in Christ as Savior.

"And after certain days, when Felix came with his wife Drusilla, which was a Jewess, he sent for Paul, and heard him concerning the faith in Christ. And as he reasoned of righteousness, temperance, and judgment to come, Felix trembled, and answered, Go thy way for this time; when I have a convenient season, I will call for thee" (Acts 24:24-25).

Although we are told that Felix trembled, he was not willing to accept Paul's message, and so sent him away. Again, we see someone left yet unsaved. Why? Was it because he was unwilling to turn from unbelief to belief in Christ? NO. Just as with the rich, young ruler, it was because Felix was faced with more than just the question of belief in Christ. He was faced with his sin and the coming judgment.

The difficulty in coming to salvation is not in just believing in Jesus; it is believing that we *need* Jesus to save us from our sins, and that he is the only hope we have of being reconciled to God and saved from a fiery eternity in

Hell. Believing merely the facts of Jesus death burial and resurrection alone does not save without repentance toward God. The simple acceptance of the facts of the person of Jesus by an unrepentant sinner does not save. Our sin is what condemned us; and it is sin that hardens us against belief.

"Take heed, brethren, lest there be in any of you an evil heart of unbelief, in departing from the living God. But exhort one another daily, while it is called To day; lest any of you be hardened through the deceitfulness of sin" (Hebrews 3:12-13).

As a child, growing up in the Catholic Church, I believed in Jesus. I believed that he was the sinless son of God who died for our sins, was buried, rose again the third day and was seated at the right hand of the Father. I even believed that he would come again someday to judge the world. I was not however, saved.

Why not? Because although I believed and trusted in Christ, I also trusted in my works to pay for the sins that I was unwilling to repent of. I was so deceived by sin, false religion and my own self-righteousness that I did not even believe that I was separated from God. The truth was, I didn't really need a Savior, because I didn't really think I was that bad. I thought I was doing alright on my own.

"When Jesus heard it, he saith unto them, They that are whole have no need of the physician, but they that are sick: I came not to call the righteous, but sinners to repentance" (Mark 2:17).

It wasn't until well into my adult life, that I finally became convicted by the Holy Spirit of God for my sins. I knew then that I was not alright on my own. I honestly feared that if Christ came back and found me where I was in my life, that I was in big trouble.

At that point I knew I needed to do something to repair my standing with God, but what? My husband and I began visiting Churches, looking for the answer. We finally settled on a Fundamental, Independent Baptist Church, where we found that answer. By then, I was well aware of my sin and inability to free myself from it. I knew that I deserved God's punishment and quickly learned that there was nothing I could do to pay for my sins on my own because they just kept piling up. It was then that I heard the truth of the gospel that Jesus Christ paid it all, that he did for me what I could not do for myself.

"For by grace are ye saved through faith; and that not of yourselves: it is the gift of God: Not of works, lest any man should boast" (Ephesians 2:8-9).

That precious verse was the final piece of the puzzle for me. That was what I needed to understand in order to truly believe in Christ alone as my Savior. For me, repentance included not only turning from sin, but also turning from dead works and false beliefs. Trusting in Christ without repentance toward God is not really trusting in Christ at all.

Are repentance and faith the same thing?

Another error of redefining repentance is the idea that repentance and faith are the same thing. This is also an attempt to justify a lack of repentance preaching.

Although repentance and faith work very closely together, they are not the same thing. This is very easily proven by scripture. Paul made it clear that our repentance is toward God while our faith is toward Christ. Repentance is that recognition of our sinful condition and separation from God, while faith in Christ is the solution. There is no salvation without both repentance and faith. One is not sufficient without the other.

It may be that we have been offered a Savior to deliver us from Hell, but have not yet become repentant, or even convicted of our sin against God. Many people attempt to receive the free gift of salvation with no desire to be reconciled to God, but instead desire to continue in sin without repentance.

Or, it may be that we are sorrowfully aware of our sin and desire to turn from it so that we might be reconciled to the God whom we have offended, (repentance) but do not necessarily have faith in Christ. We may not even know of Christ, much like Cornelius or the disciples of John.

"There was a certain man in Caesarea called Cornelius, a centurion of the band called the Italian band, A devout man, and one that feared God with all his house, which gave much alms to the people, and prayed to God alway. He saw in a vision evidently about the ninth hour of the day an angel of God coming in to him, and saying unto him, Cornelius. And when he looked on him, he was afraid, and said, What is it, Lord? And he said unto him, Thy prayers and thine alms are come up for a memorial before God. And now send men to Joppa, and call for one Simon, whose surname is Peter: He lodgeth with one Simon a tanner, whose house is by the sea side: he shall tell thee what thou oughtest to do" (Acts 10:1-6).

Cornelius believed in God and desired to have a relationship with him. He worshipped and prayed to God and did alms, but did not know how to be truly reconciled to God because although he had a repentant heart, he had not yet heard the gospel of Jesus Christ. God sent Peter to preach to him, so that he might be saved.

"And he commanded us to preach unto the people, and to testify that it is he which was ordained of God to be the Judge of quick and dead. To him give all the prophets witness, that through his name whosoever believeth in him shall receive remission of sins. While Peter yet spake these words, the Holy Ghost fell on all them which heard the word. And they of the circumcision which believed were astonished, as many as came with Peter, because that on the Gentiles also was poured out the gift of the Holy Ghost. For they heard them speak with tongues, and magnify God. Then answered Peter, Can any man forbid water, that these should not be baptized, which have received the Holy Ghost as well as we?" (Acts 10:42-47).

Notice also that "while Peter yet spake", the Holy Ghost fell upon them. They were not led through a sinner's prayer, or even to make a verbal profession, and yet the Holy Ghost came upon them, and immediately they were baptized.

"So then faith cometh by hearing, and hearing by the word of God" (Romans 10:17).

Let's look at another instance where repentance toward God was evidenced, but faith in Christ was not.

"And it came to pass, that, while Apollos was at Corinth, Paul having passed through the upper coasts came to Ephesus: and finding certain disciples, He said unto them, Have ye received the Holy Ghost since ye believed? And they said unto him, We have not so much as heard whether there be any Holy Ghost. And he said unto them, Unto what then were ye baptized? And they said, Unto John's baptism. Then said Paul, John verily baptized with the baptism of repentance, saying unto the people, that they should believe on him which should come after him, that is, on Christ Jesus. When they heard this, they were baptized in the name of the Lord Jesus" (Acts 19:1-5).

These believers were baptized unto John's baptism of repentance toward God, but had not heard the gospel of Jesus Christ. Once they were told of Christ, these repentant sinners readily believed, and were baptized in the name of Christ.

Offering Christ to an *un*repentant sinner who has no interest in being reconciled to God however, has no meaning. Unbelief in Christ is at its core, unbelief in God, his declared righteousness, and just judgement of sin-

not simply a rejection of Christ, as many choose to present it.

You may have heard it preached this way, "What will you do with Christ?" It is often suggested that this is the greatest question in life. To those who have no regard for God and no desire to repent, the question of what they will do with Christ is ridiculous because they have no need for Christ. Rejection of Christ is the natural result of that mindset.

Without understanding his condemnation, a lost sinner cannot embrace the one who can save him from that condemnation- therefore the gospel of Christ is only foolishness to him. It is this rejection of God and his rule of man that must be repented of. Once man recognizes God's righteous rule, his own condemnation and repents, embracing Christ is the only logical option.

That is why repentance is toward our perfect and holy God who we have sinned against and whose wrath we will face one day if we die in our lost condition. It is God who we are separated from because of our sin, and who desires to be reconciled to us. He desires it so much that he made provision himself for the payment of our sins. He sent his only son to pay the penalty we deserve, so that we can be reconciled to him.

> "But without faith it is impossible to please him: for he that cometh to God must believe that he is, and that he is a rewarder of them that diligently seek him" (Hebrews 11:6).

Why repentance is so important

It is only through recognition of this hopeless, helpless predicament as condemned sinners that we can even comprehend our need for a Savior, let alone have faith in him.

Repentance and faith work so closely together that it would be easy to misunderstand their relationship and possibly even think that they are the same, but scripture shows us over and over how repentance prepares the way for faith. Throughout the Bible, we see how God used one thing to prepare the way for another.

The Old Testament prepared the way for the New Testament.

> "Then said he, Lo, I come to do thy will, O God. He taketh away the first, that he may establish the second" (Hebrews 10:9).

The Old Testament was for our teaching and admonition, to teach us about God and prepare us for the salvation that would come to all.

The law prepared the way for grace.

"Therefore by the deeds of the law there shall no flesh be justified in his sight: for by the law is the knowledge of sin" (Romans 3:20).

Only through the knowledge of our sin can we appreciate God's grace and mercy towards us.

John the Baptist prepared the way for Christ.

"And he shall go before him in the spirit and power of Elias, to turn the hearts of the fathers to the children, and the disobedient to the wisdom of the just; to make ready a people prepared for the Lord" (Luke 1:17).

John the Baptist was "The voice of one crying in the wilderness, Prepare ye the way of the Lord, make his paths straight" (Mark 1:3). He preached repentance toward God, (straightening out the crooked, froward path and breaking up the fallow ground of the heart) in preparation of the Lord's coming.
Why? Because "faith cometh by hearing, and hearing by the word of God" (Romans 10:17), but the word of faith cannot take root in a stony heart hardened by sin! The heart of man must be prepared to receive the Lord.

"When any one heareth the word of the kingdom, and understandeth it not, then cometh the wicked one, and catcheth away that which was sown in his heart. This is he which received seed by the way side. But he that received the seed into stony places, the same is he that heareth the word, and anon with joy receiveth it; Yet hath he not root in himself, but dureth for a while: for when tribulation or persecution ariseth because of the word, by and by he is offended. He also that received seed among the thorns is he that heareth the word; and the care of this world, and the deceitfulness of riches, choke the word, and he becometh unfruitful. But he that received seed into the good ground is he that heareth the word, and understandeth it; which also beareth fruit, and bringeth forth, some an hundredfold, some sixty, some thirty" (Matthew 13:19-23).

That is why we are admonished to take heed how we hear. If our hearts are hardened with sin against God, how can we possibly expect to receive His word into it? We must receive His word "...with all readiness of mind..." (Acts 17:11), as Bereans, first believing God and that His word is truth.

"Take heed therefore how ye hear: for whosoever hath, to him shall be given; and whosoever hath not, from him shall be taken even that which he seemeth to have" (Luke 8:18).

Repentance toward God prepares the way for faith in Christ.

"And saying, The time is fulfilled, and the kingdom of God is at hand: repent ye, and believe the gospel" (Mark 1:15).

Through the fall, man is spiritually dead, and his soul (the seat of his emotions and his will; the place of his decision making) now dwells within his decaying mortal body as a defenseless prisoner, controlled by its sinful desires. Though he would repent, his conscience recognizing and bearing record of his sin as an offense to God; he cannot overcome his sin. Within himself he has no power to break free from the sin that keeps him in bondage. Repentance simply cannot save him from his sins, nor pay the penalty they bring.

"For they that are after the flesh do mind the things of the flesh; but they that are after the Spirit the things of the Spirit. For to be carnally minded is death; but to be spiritually minded is life and peace. Because the carnal mind is enmity against God: for it is not subject to the law of God, neither indeed can be. So then they that are in the flesh cannot please God. But ye are not in the flesh, but in the Spirit, if so be that the Spirit of God dwell in you. Now if any man have not the Spirit of Christ, he is none of his" (Romans 8:5-9).

In our flesh, we cannot please God. Our repentance, although commanded cannot save us but is simply an acknowledgement of our sinful condition and a willingness to turn to God.

Repentant man finds that he must look outside himself for help to overcome and atone for his sin. It is that desire to change and understanding of his own corruption that drives him to his knees. That is when the gospel truly begins to make sense. That is when it is no longer foolishness, but the answer to life's greatest question. It is then that he looks in faith to the sinless Savior, who alone can do for him what he could not do for himself, that is to save him from the power and the penalty of sin.

Through faith, he receives the precious gift of salvation God offers through his son, Jesus Christ. With salvation in Christ, his soul is freed from the bondage of sin within his flesh, and he is empowered with the life giving, indwelling Spirit of God, enabling him to overcome the sins which once held him bound.

"Not by works of righteousness which we have done, but according to his mercy he saved us, by the washing of regeneration, and renewing of the Holy Ghost" (Titus 3:5).

"The law- having done its work, convincing man of his sin and leaving him no more able to argue against God- leaves him guilty before God. Humble, contrite and repentant of his self-righteousness, and dead works, he now turns to God, willing to be reconciled to him and to hear the words of life that minister faith unto him. Wandering out of the darkened, twisted trail of self-effort, he finds himself finally on a straight path prepared by the Lord. His mouth stopped, he begins to take in God's word. It pierces his heart again and again as he hears of his condemnation before a holy God. The punishment for his sins, separation from God in a flaming Hell, he now sees as just and deserved.

His broken heart mourns in agony over his past sins and lost condition, seeing how his sin has separated him from God. His heart melts within him as his sorrow and anguish endure beyond what he thinks he can bear. This is where God meets man and is ever ready to show him mercy. He hears finally the good news of the gospel, how 'that Christ died for our sins according to the scriptures and that he was buried and rose again the third day according to the scriptures' (1Corinthians 15:3). He knows that he has heard it all before, but this time, somehow it's different. It might just be the answer to everything." *Seasons of Life: Man's Journey from the Garden to Glory*- Sandra M. Platt

Repentance brings us to the point of need, making us ready & willing to turn to God to receive the faith that cometh by hearing. When we repent of our sins we become willing to hear the words of life that minister faith to us. Through that faith in Christ, we are born again. We must preach repentance!

CHAPTER 3
EASY BELIEVEISM: ANOTHER GOSPEL

Most Christians have heard of Easy Believeism and are aware of its negative connotation. Many are not completely sure what it is; but if it's bad, they sure aren't doing it! When questioned about their stand they will almost always deny participation in it, even when they rely solely upon it for their Evangelism. They may even agree that *there is NO magic prayer* (while they consistently use it as such). I would like to believe though, that it is not a desire to deceive which prompts their denial, but simply an ignorance of what is truly meant by Easy Believe-ism.

The primary reason most do not acknowledge participating in Easy Believeism, is simply because they don't know it *as* Easy Believeism. To them, it's called *leading someone to the Lord* or *soul-winning* (which usually translates to preaching a shallow gospel message, successfully convincing someone to pray the sinner's prayer and then offering assurance of their salvation based on such).

Most who use this method of Evangelism sincerely believe that what they are practicing is genuine, biblical soul-winning because that is what they were taught. Even those who do realize something is wrong with these methods, just don't know what else to do. This is NOT Bible evangelism and this message is not the gospel. This is Easy Believeism.

When confronted with the error of these methods, many defensively reject what they perceive to be the *wrong* in Anti-Easy Believeism arguments even suggesting that any who reject Easy Believeism are condemning soul-winning and the responsibility to lead others to the Lord. They even suggest that by questioning the validity of their methods, we are condemning their converts to Hell. This accusation however is false. It is the desire to see souls truly saved that prompts the demand for biblical methods of Evangelism.

Obviously, it is not pointing out the error of Easy Believe-ism that sends them to Hell. These straw man arguments are often systematically dismantled, while the heart of Easy Believeism remains unaddressed. Clearly, there must be some confusion.

What exactly is Easy Believeism?

Easy Believeism is a method of evangelism that focuses primarily on getting people to pray a prayer. The reciting of such a prayer is generally viewed as evidence of faith and the prayer itself as a means of securing salvation. It has been suggested that Easy Believeism would be better called

Easy Prayerism because of its over-emphasis on prayer.

After being given a shallow gospel message which either minimizes or excludes repentance altogether, the converts are typically asked if they want to go to Heaven when they die. Since most people with any sense at all do desire to go to Heaven, it is not difficult to then lead them through the sinner's prayer. Those who do repeat the prayer are immediately assured of their salvation.

This positive message, of simply *ask Jesus into your heart* if you want to go to Heaven seems so much more appealing, that no longer do we burden people with the biblical gospel and its negative message of repentance once preached by the apostle Paul.

"And how I kept back nothing that was profitable unto you, but have shewed you, and have taught you publickly, and from house to house, Testifying both to the Jews, and also to the Greeks, repentance toward God, and faith toward our Lord Jesus Christ" (Acts 20:20-21).

The message of reconciliation to God has been replaced with *simply ask Jesus into your heart* (most often, your sinful and continuously rebellious heart). No turning from sin, no desire to be reconciled with God, and no genuine need of a Savior is even required in this new gospel. It is usually kept very positive in order to make it more attractive.

No longer do we dare to plow the soil of men's hearts with the preaching of the fear of the Lord. No longer do we sow the seed of the sincere word of God, nor do we even water it, and yet we insist that we reap souls instantly. We refuse to be led by the Spirit, but instead run far ahead. No longer are we content to allow God to give the increase, but choose instead to make our own converts and seal them with a prayer rather than with the regeneration of the Holy Spirit.

So positive and easy is our message, that we promise lost souls forgiveness and eternal life, in return for just repeating a prayer, even if they display little or no interest in God. A mere desire to go to Heaven is all we ask.

In my own Church, our Pastor is very clear in preaching that a profession without regeneration is worthless. He emphasizes the need to be born again as the true evidence of salvation, and not merely the profession. With almost every testimony he hears, of those who are said to have been saved, he prays that that testimony is sincere. Why? Because we know that most are not.

Although most all of us know and even admit that the majority of professions *are* insincere and often coerced, we lead them to believe that this profession of theirs has indeed secured salvation. Then we assure them of their newly acquired salvation and counsel them to never question it.

Who are we to do and say such things? How could we ever come to the place where we would make such claims as though we have the power to administer salvation and guarantee it with our man-made prayer?

Most Fundamental Bible believing Christians would immediately refute the Pope's, or anyone else's claims to pronounce salvation (or damnation) upon anyone. They would quickly cite: "For there is one God, and one mediator between God and men, the man Christ Jesus" (1 Timothy 2:5.)

They would also insist that biblical salvation is not obtained by works done by men, but only by faith.

"For by grace are ye saved through faith; and that not of yourselves: it is the gift of God: Not of works, lest any man should boast" (Ephesians 2:8).

They would be absolutely right on both accounts, and yet when it comes to evangelism, they themselves claim that same power, pronouncing salvation upon any who follow after their own prescribed works (praying a prayer).

Have we now become the mediators of salvation, to be initiated upon our own direction? Can we ever know with certainty who has true faith? How can we make that determination for someone else, and then suggest that a simple prayer is their initiation into Christianity?

"Not by works of righteousness which we have done, but according to his mercy he saved us, by the washing of regeneration, and renewing of the Holy Ghost" (Titus 3:5).

No true salvation has ever been sealed by a prayer, but ONLY by the Holy Spirit of God.

"Who hath also sealed us, and given the earnest of the Spirit in our hearts" (2 Corinthians 1:22).

"...Now if any man have not the Spirit of Christ, he is none of his" (Romans 8:9).

What's wrong with the Sinner's prayer?

While praying is not wrong, and even praying a sinner's prayer as a means of confessing the faith that is already in your heart, is not in itself wrong either; the tendency to view this prayer as a guarantee of salvation certainly is wrong.

Although there are no biblical accounts whatsoever of praying to receive salvation, it is now commonly taught that in order to be saved, one must call upon the name of the Lord through prayer. Many equate this *call* with reciting a sinner's prayer, asking Christ to save them. This idea is loosely based on Romans 10

> "That if thou shalt confess with thy mouth the Lord Jesus, and shalt believe in thine heart that God hath raised him from the dead, thou shalt be saved. For with the heart man believeth unto righteousness; and with the mouth confession is made unto salvation. For the scripture saith, Whosoever believeth on him shall not be ashamed. For there is no difference between the Jew and the Greek: for the same Lord over all is rich unto all that call upon him. For whosoever shall call upon the name of the Lord shall be saved" (Romans 10:9-13).

Because of this, the sinner's prayer is now viewed as a *means* of entering into salvation. But, is this consistent with Bible teaching? Is this even the message conveyed through this passage of scripture?

This certainly would seem to be in contradiction with the salvation *by grace through faith* that we as Bible believers claim to believe. Does the Bible teach justification by faith *and* a verbal confession? or by faith alone? Are we saved by grace through faith *and* prayer? or merely by faith?

Does the Bible really tell us that we must pray and ask Christ to save us? If not, then we may be in danger of serious error. Adding requirements to salvation that the Bible does not spell out is no less than adding works to the gospel. If the Bible does NOT tell sinners that they must pray to be saved, then are we not guilty of preaching "another gospel"?

This practice certainly was not used by Jesus, nor by any of the apostles. As a matter of fact, it was not even used by the early Church Fathers, but only came into use in the early 1900's.

During Christ's time on earth, we are told of many which came to faith in him, but *none* that were commanded by him to pray in order to receive salvation.

To the sinful woman who washed his feet with her hair, Jesus simply said: "… Thy faith hath saved thee; go in peace" (Luke 7:50). There is nothing to indicate that she prayed any prayer or asked him to save her, but only her faith is mentioned here.

To the woman with the issue of blood, who reached out and touched his garment he said: "Daughter, be of good comfort; thy faith hath made thee whole" (Matthew 9:22). Again, there is no indication that she had said a prayer of any sort.

The Samaritan woman at the well was saved while speaking with the Lord, and yet, once again no prayer is mentioned and no asking him into her heart or life. (John 4:1-42) The list could go on and on of conversions described in the Bible, by Christ as well as by the Apostles: Zaccheus, the centurion's servant, the man who was sick with palsy, whose friends brought him to Christ...etc.

Repentant faith is certainly described in all of these accounts, but not a word is ever recorded about a sinner's prayer or any prayer at all being used as a means of receiving salvation.

When we read the account of the conversion of Cornelius and those who were gathered together with him, we are told that "While Peter yet spake these words, the Holy Ghost fell on all them which heard the word" (Acts 10:33).

It tells us that while Peter was yet speaking, through the hearing of the word, they believed in Christ as Savior and yet no verbal call was made. No sinner's prayer was prayed, or any other prayer, because Peter had not yet even concluded his sermon and yet by faith they entered into salvation.

Peter immediately instructed them to be baptized.

"Can any man forbid water, that these should not be baptized, which have received the Holy Ghost as well as we? And he commanded them to be baptized in the name of the Lord" (Acts 10: 47-48).

We see this same type of salvation experience: "Howbeit many of them which heard the word believed; and the number of the men was about five thousand" (Acts 4:4).

"So then faith cometh by hearing, and hearing by the word of God" (Romans 10:17).

If, as the Bible tells us, salvation can be received without a verbal *call* or sinner's prayer, then how are we to understand this scripture in Romans that tells us:

"That if thou shalt confess with thy mouth the Lord Jesus, and shalt believe in thine heart that God hath raised him from the dead, thou shalt be saved. For with the heart man believeth unto righteousness; and with the mouth confession is made unto salvation" (Romans 10:9-10).

Looking at these verses can seem a bit confusing at first. Since confessing the Lord is first listed in this passage of scripture, it might seem to suggest that the order of salvation would be this: that 1st we confess the Lord Jesus with our mouth, and 2nd, believe in our hearts that God hath raised him from the dead. This could understandably lead some to believe that the confession of the mouth is key in receiving salvation.

But, when we get to verse ten, the order is reversed. Now it states that with the heart, we believe unto righteousness, and then with our mouth confession is made unto salvation.

So, which is the means of obtaining salvation? Confession or belief? With the heart we believe unto righteousness. We are made righteous before God through belief in Christ. Verse 11 begins to clarify it for us:

11 "For the scripture saith, Whosoever believeth on him shall not be ashamed."

Whosoever believeth in him, not whosoever *confesseth*. This is further illustrated in the following scriptures.

"For whosoever shall call upon the name of the Lord shall be saved. How then shall they call on him in whom they have not believed? and how shall they believe in him of whom they have not heard? and how shall they hear without a preacher? And how shall they preach, except they be sent? as it is written, How beautiful are the feet of them that preach the gospel of peace, and bring glad tidings of good things!" (Romans 10:13-15).

It does indeed say that whosoever calls upon the name of the Lord shall be saved, but then it asks: how can they call if they have not believed? How can they believe if they have not heard? (remember, faith cometh by hearing.) They cannot call, without first believing. Simply calling upon the name of the Lord does NOT secure salvation, but only belief.

This shows us clearly that belief must come first and is the sole means of justification, NOT confessing. The Bible consistently teaches that the means of salvation is by repentant faith in Jesus Christ, alone.

True belief will result in salvation and will at some point produce a profession, but a lack of profession initially does not in any way prevent salvation. Salvation is by grace through faith, *not* through a verbal profession. Where then does the confession with the mouth come into play? The confession of the Lord Jesus Christ as Savior is the **result** of salvation.

"for of the abundance of the heart his mouth speaketh" (Luke 6:45).

True salvation will show in our verbal conversation and in our lives. It is not the means of justification, but the testimony of justification. A true believer will show a testimony of Christ. It is much the same as with baptism.

30

"He that believeth and is baptized shall be saved…" (Mark 16:16a).

When we read that whoever believes and is baptized shall be saved, initially we might think that salvation hinges upon baptism as well as belief, but again, the latter part of the verse tells us: "but he that believeth not shall be damned" (Mark 16:16b).

We can easily see here again that salvation hinges upon belief and belief alone. Belief is the sole means of salvation, and it is that without which, man cannot receive salvation.

Just as it is not baptism upon which salvation hinges, but belief; so it is not confessing Christ which saves, but belief.

Telling people that they need to pray a prayer to be saved is no different than telling them that they need to be baptized to be saved.

It is *not* the calling upon the name of the Lord that saves, but belief. Calling upon the name of the Lord is a phrase frequently used in the Old Testament, but used only once here in the New Testament.

In the Old Testament, it was not used as a onetime verbal call for entrance into salvation, but was used to describe an acknowledgement and submission to God's ways. When men called upon the name of the Lord in the Old Testament it was as a willing association with God as his follower.

According to Strong's concordance of the Bible, the *phrase* to call upon the name of the Lord, is:

> an expression finding its explanation in the fact that prayers addressed to God ordinarily began with an invocation of the divine name, Jehovah. (Strong's Greek Lexicon "G1941 - epikaleō - Strong's Greek Lexicon (KJV)." Blue Letter Bible. Accessed 5 Mar, 2017.)

In the Old Testament, it was basically a turning to Jehovah God (in repentance) to be reconciled with him. In the New Testament, this is accomplished through faith in his son, Jesus Christ.

Whosoever shall call upon the name of the Lord, or in other words: whosoever shall willingly be reconciled to God by his appointed means of justification, which is through belief in Jesus Christ his son, shall be saved. It is NOT a call or prayer that saves, nor even the *willing association* of ourselves with Jesus Christ as his disciples, but faith alone. There IS NO magic prayer that saves.

Deciding to pray a prayer or call on the name of the Lord is no guarantee that we are saved. There must be true belief within the heart for that profession to be real. A profession without faith is worthless, not magical. Not everyone who calls upon the name of the Lord does so in genuine faith in our Savior. Jesus made that clear.

> "Not every one that saith unto me, Lord, Lord, shall enter into the kingdom of heaven; but he that doeth the will of my Father which is in heaven. Many will say to me in that day, Lord, Lord, have we not prophesied in thy name? and in thy name have cast out devils? and in thy name done many wonderful works? And then will I profess unto them, I never knew you: depart from me, ye that work iniquity" (Matthew 7:21-23.)

To confess with thy mouth the Lord Jesus means to testify of the belief that you already have. A sinner's prayer asking Jesus into your heart is not a biblical interpretation of testifying to the saving faith that is already there. Simply calling upon the Lord's name with an expectation of being saved and receiving faith afterward is also not the same thing.

But what if they don't make a profession? I have heard some insist that we must *seal the deal*. It is not our job, our even within our capability to seal the deal for them. That responsibility and power belongs ONLY to the Holy Spirit of God. Again, when did we become the mediators or salvation? When did salvation become something that could be initiated upon our command our leading?

We are told to simply preach the gospel. We are never told to seal the deal. God tells us that he will do that. Will we trust God to do what he says we will do, or will we continue to do what seems right in our own eyes?

If we don't lead them through a prayer and pronounce them saved, then what are we to do?

Looking at Bible accounts of salvation may give us some light. How were Christians saved under the apostles' preaching? In the book of Acts, we read that when the apostles preached the word of God, the hearers, believing the word preached, were convicted by the Holy Spirit, and moved to ask "what shall we do?" (Acts 2:37)

The answer might surprise you. Peter did NOT say, "simply pray this prayer after me", or even, "ask Jesus into your heart."

> "Then Peter said unto them, Repent, and be baptized every one of you in the name of Jesus Christ for the remission of sins, and ye shall receive the gift of the Holy Ghost" (Acts 2:38).

Throughout the Bible, the answer is always "repent and believe" and be baptized as a public profession of your faith in Christ. Nowhere in the Bible was anyone instructed to pray a prayer or told that they were saved because they did so, yet we are told in detail of many salvations. How did they know that these were saved? We can never really know someone else's salvation with certainty, but the Bible gives us some evidences that we can look for. On the day of Pentecost, we read that when believers were saved, they obeyed what Peter told them to do.

> "Then they that gladly received his word were baptized: and the same day there were added unto them about three thousand souls. And they continued stedfastly in the apostles' doctrine and fellowship, and in breaking of bread, and in prayers" (Acts 2:41-42).

If they are saved, they *will* confess that through their words and through their lives! If the heart truly believes, the mouth will confess it without our prompting. No preset words or prayer will be necessary. And if they truly possess saving faith, they will be saved. Nothing we do or fail to do will change that.

I know that many of your reading this right now are asking, "but what if the Devil steals it away before they get saved?" Look at the parable of the sower once more:

> "Hear ye therefore the parable of the sower. When any one heareth the word of the kingdom, and understandeth it not, then cometh the wicked one, and catcheth away that which was sown in his heart. This is he which received seed by the way side" (Matthew 13:18).

If the Devil can steal it, then it isn't faith.

If the Devil comes and takes away the seed, it means that it has not yet taken root. They do not yet possess true faith. This seed was cast by the wayside and not even understood. The wayside is a description of a traveled road or path. In farming, it would be the path the farmer walked upon to throw seed onto the good soil. As he walked he would pack down the soil under his feet, hardening it with every step. This ground would not easily receive seed, or allow it to take root and grow into faith. The seed would remain on top of the hard ground for the birds to come and steal away.

Those who received the seed by the way side have hearts that are still too hardened for the gospel to penetrate. Only repentance toward God can break through that hard soil. Trying to lead them through a sinner's prayer before the Devil steals it away would do them no good if true faith has not yet even grown in their heart. If true faith is not there, it may lead them to a false assurance and in essence seal their condemnation instead of their salvation.

If, on the other hand, someone did have true saving faith and we *failed* to lead them through a prayer, that faith would still save them. Remember? We are saved *by grace through faith*, **not** through a prayer.

When Peter spoke to Cornelius and all those with him, they were saved before he even finished speaking. They made no profession of faith and yet they were saved.

It is not our job, or even within our capability to seal their salvation. Only the Holy Spirit can do that. Our job is to preach the gospel, and trust the Lord for the results. If we change nothing else, we must at the *very least* stop leading people to believe they have been saved just because they've said a sinner's prayer!

We *are* responsible for creating false converts through our Easy Believeism gospel.

We make it far too easy for someone (especially children), without faith to make a meaningless profession by using terminology that is misleadingly. We tell people to make a decision to *accept Jesus* or to *ask him into their heart*.

I have heard many try to explain away their responsibility in false conversions by suggesting that if someone tells *them* they are saved, then all they can do is believe it since they cannot see their heart. That is true except that with Easy Believeism/Prayerism, it is generally not the new convert proclaiming salvation, but the overly zealous soul-winner.

We cannot in any degree of honesty, lead someone to believe that making a decision or praying a prayer saves them, put the words in their mouths, write their names in the back of our Bibles, congratulate them on getting saved, and then deny any responsibility for their false conversions.

What's even worse is that most soul-winners do not stop at merely suggesting that salvation has been secured by a profession or a prayer. Most will go as far as giving the new convert an *assurance* that they are indeed saved and saved eternally, instructing them to hold fast to their profession in times of doubt and to never question the validity of their salvation.

It absolutely amazes me that we are so reluctant to tell anyone that they may not be saved because *we can't see their hearts-only God can*, and yet we would dare tell them (again, not being able to see their hearts) that they are saved simply because we coerced them into praying a prayer. Did it never occur to us that telling people who are not saved that they are may be sending them to Hell? (While telling someone who is saved that they may not be, can do them no spiritual harm at all.)

If we tell people that all they have to do is say a prayer to be saved, then they say the prayer, but for whatever reason they aren't really saved, is that anything less than a lie? Can we even possibly say that we are not responsible for their false conversion?

Why would we assure someone that they can trust their souls to a mere profession when the Bible does not say that? The Bible warns over and over of those who are deceived and admonishes believers to "examine yourselves, whether ye be in the faith: prove your own selves" (2 Corinthians 13:5).

Only they themselves and God can know. Instead of our own worthless guarantees, we should be pointing them to the holy scriptures with which they can examine themselves by to see if they are in the faith. The book of 1John for instance gives many evidences of the indwelling Holy Spirit with which to examine yourself by.

"The wind bloweth where it listeth, and thou hearest the sound thereof, but canst not tell whence it cometh, and whither it goeth: so is every one that is born of the Spirit" (John 3:8).

It is so vitally important for us to understand that we cannot ever really know for sure whether someone has truly been saved, or know at what moment salvation has occurred in them. Only God knows who is truly saved, and who is not and only God knows and can determine the moment when the Holy Spirit quickens them. The only evidence we have of someone's salvation is the fruit that results from their rebirth. These may not be immediately evident, or they may have an outward appearance of salvation, that does not last.

When Jesus walked the Earth, many people chose to follow him initially, but as the trials came the crowds grew smaller & smaller & many fell away. "From that time many of his disciples went back, and walked no more with him. Then said Jesus unto the twelve, Will ye also go away?" (John 6:66- 67)

We should never assure people of salvation merely because of a profession.

Replacing Baptism with a Sinner's prayer

Many of those who profess belief never even go as far as being baptized. Is that not the very first evidence we should see in those who profess? If we were looking at the Bible for our examples, then certainly we would. Granted, some may have limitations such as the thief on the cross, or health or imprisonment; but for those who do not, we should expect them to publicly testify of the salvation we are claiming for them, just as we saw in the early Church.

How did we get to the place where do not even expect this anymore? The problem is that we no longer look to the Bible to teach us, but instead to the famous Evangelists that claimed great results.

In the 1800's the anxious bench, (originally called the mourner's bench) was made famous by Charles Finney and used as a way of encouraging those who might have spiritual interest, to make a physical response by coming forward. Those who came forward were then counseled and counted as salvations. The modern equivalent is today's altar call, where those who come forward are led through a sinner's prayer and counted as saved. That is why Charles Finney is sometimes called *the Father of the Altar call.*

I was shocked and horrified when I read what Finney had to say about it:

"The Church has always felt it necessary to have something of this kind to answer this very purpose. In the days of the apostles, baptism answered this purpose. The gospel was preached to the people, and then all those who were willing to be on the side of Christ, were called out to be baptized. It (baptism) held the place that the anxious seat does now as a public manifestation of their determination to be Christians."- Charles Grandison Finney, Hindrances to Revival (1792-1875).

What unbelievable nerve to say such a thing! To treat baptism as merely something to satisfy the demands of the Church, rather than the command of God is horrific. To even suggest that we could substitute our own man made inventions for the commands of God is unparalleled arrogance. Baptism is commanded by God as a public testimony of our salvation in Jesus Christ. Of course, we know that baptism does not save but it is commanded by God!

What's even worse, is that we have all bought it! Today, we accept the sinner's prayer as the public testimony and signifying act of salvation. We pronounce any saved who simply repeat a scripted prayer. Often, we do not even mention baptism, probably because the majority of those professing through sinner's prayers never even make it to Church. This is NOT biblical evangelism!

How dare we substitute a sinner's prayer for baptism? Jesus Christ himself submitted to baptism. Why? To fulfil all righteousness.

"And Jesus answering said unto him, Suffer it to be so now: for thus it becometh us to fulfil all righteousness. Then he suffered him" (Matthew 3:15).

Obviously, baptism was important to Christ. Shouldn't it be important to us as well? Jesus was completely obedient to God and always did that which was pleasing to God. He came to fulfil every word of God, to perform perfectly the will of his Father. If Christ himself submitted to it, how dare we think so little of this command to replace it with our own methods?

When we are baptized in the name of Jesus Christ, we are associating ourselves with Christ. We go down under the water and come back up picturing his death, burial and resurrection and our new life in Him. Neither the anxious bench nor the sinner's prayer can picture that and neither of those can fulfill the command of God. We are commanded by Jesus to go and preach the gospel and baptize believers, and then teach them (make disciples), not simply go and lead them through a prayer.

> "Go ye therefore, and teach all nations, baptizing them in the name of the Father, and of the Son, and of the Holy Ghost: Teaching them to observe all things whatsoever I have commanded you: and, lo, I am with you alway, even unto the end of the world. Amen" (Matthew 28:19-20).

We are NOT fulfilling the great commission by simply going and leading people through prayers and yet we act as though we are and applaud every sinner's prayer as such. We need to get back to the Bible. We need to look to the Apostles for our doctrine, rather than the "Great Evangelists".

> "Then Peter said unto them, Repent, and be baptized every one of you in the name of Jesus Christ for the remission of sins, and ye shall receive the gift of the Holy Ghost" (Acts 2:38).

> "Then they that gladly received his word were baptized: and the same day there were added unto them about three thousand souls"(Acts 2:41).

> "But when they believed Philip preaching the things concerning the kingdom of God, and the name of Jesus Christ, they were baptized, both men and women" (Acts 8:12).

> "Then Simon himself believed also: and when he was baptized, he continued with Philip, and wondered, beholding the miracles and signs which were done. Acts 8:16 (For as yet he was fallen upon none of them: only they were baptized in the name of the Lord Jesus.)" (Acts 8:13).

> "And as they went on their way, they came unto a certain water: and the eunuch said, See, here is water; what doth hinder me to be baptized?" (Acts 8:36).

If we counted our converts according to biblical evidences rather than by sinner's prayers, our numbers would be dramatically different.

"Then they that gladly received his word were baptized: and the same day there were added unto them about three thousand souls. And they continued stedfastly in the apostles' doctrine and fellowship, and in breaking of bread, and in prayers" (Acts 2:41-42).

If we did NOT answer the question of, "what shall we do to be saved?" with "say this prayer"; but instead gave the biblical command to repent and believe, and admonished those who believed to be baptized as a testimony of their faith, how many of those would follow through? How many would be added to the Church and continue steadfastly in the apostles' doctrine, fellowship and prayer?

I would suspect that it would only be a tiny fraction of those we claim salvation for today. Sadly, the vast majority of our converts do not show any biblical evidences of salvation, yet we promise them eternal life in return for their prayer. The sinner's prayer is NOT an accurate measure of salvations!

Our converts generally continue to live in unrepentant sin, unchanged, yet now shaming the name of Christ by their professions.

"They profess that they know God; but in works they deny him, being abominable, and disobedient, and unto every good work reprobate" (Titus 1:16).

"He that saith, I know him, and keepeth not his commandments, is a liar, and the truth is not in him" (1 John 2:4).

Those who do manage to come to Church, generally stay but a while, then eventually return to their old ways. Is it really any wonder? How many scriptures would we have to ignore and lies would we have to believe to convince ourselves that these obviously unregenerate false converts are better off for having heard our Easy Believeism gospel?

Some argue that "at least a few of our converts really do get saved." The percentage of those who do, is so small in comparison to the number who are not, that we simply cannot justify it. If we lead one hundred people through prayers, and only two are truly saved, while the rest are now clinging to a false assurance of salvation and unknowingly continuing toward destruction, how can we possibly think we have done right? We have helped to secure their place in Hell. These who were lost are now fatally deceived.

If a Pharmaceutical company were to advertise a new drug which is known to heal only two out of every one hundred patients, while the rest of the patients suffer fatal reactions, we would view them as criminally negligent to even continue this drug. Can we really justify continuing our false practices? If we would hold others accountable, do we not think God will hold us accountable as well? Should we not be doubly concerned when we are dealing with souls?

A Call to Examination

Below are comparisons of the claims of Easy Believeism with the word of God.

Easy Believeism: Tells the unsaved to admit that they are sinners, or confess their sin.
Bible: Tells us to repent. Anyone can admit to being a sinner, or even confess their sins and not be repentant. Catholics confess their sins regularly. This is in no way the same as repentance.

"And saying, Repent ye: for the kingdom of heaven is at hand" (Matthew 3:2).

"From that time Jesus began to preach, and to say, Repent: for the kingdom of heaven is at hand" (Matthew 4:17).

"Then Peter said unto them, Repent, an d be baptized every one of you in the name of Jesus Christ for the remission of sins, and ye shall receive the gift of the Holy Ghost" (Acts 2:38).

Easy Believeism: Instructs converts to never doubt their salvation. Many soul-winners will instruct the new convert to write down the day they prayed a prayer and hold fast to that in times of doubt.
Bible: Instructs us to examine ourselves to be sure we are in the faith, and lists many proofs of the evidence of the indwelling Holy Spirit, as well as evidences of deception. (see 1John)

"Examine yourselves, whether ye be in the faith; prove your own selves" 2 (Corinthians 13:5).

"… work out your own salvation with fear and trembling" (Philippians 2:12).

Easy Believeism: Omits, or distorts repentance so that the way of salvation is plenty broad enough for MANY to enter in (along with their false beliefs, sin, and self-righteousness).

Bible: Declares that salvation is the narrow way.

"Enter ye in at the strait gate: for wide is the gate, and broad is the way, that leadeth to destruction, and many there be which go in thereat: Because strait is the gate, and narrow is the way, which leadeth unto life, and few there be that find it" (Matthew 7:13-14).

Easy Believeism: Promises salvation to all who *profess* belief.
Bible: The Bible tells us of many who profess to believe, but are not truly saved.

"They profess that they know God; but in works they deny him, being abominable, and disobedient, and unto every good work reprobate" (Titus 1:16).

"Not every one that saith unto me, Lord, Lord, shall enter into the kingdom of heaven; but he that doeth the will of my Father which is in heaven. Many will say to me in that day, Lord, Lord, have we not prophesied in thy name? and in thy name have cast out devils? and in thy name done many wonderful works? And then will I profess unto them, I never knew you: depart from me, ye that work iniquity" (Matthew 7:21-23).

Easy Believeism: Promotes a means of salvation reduced to a mechanical device (work)-the act of saying a prayer.
Bible: Does not anywhere even suggest the use of a prayer in salvation.

"Not by works of righteousness which we have done, but according to his mercy he saved us, by the washing of regeneration, and renewing of the Holy Ghost" (Titus 3:5).

"For by grace are ye saved through faith; and that not of yourselves: it is the gift of God: Not of works, lest any man should boast" (Ephesians 2:8-9).

Easy Believeism: Offers assurance of salvation based merely upon a profession or sinner's prayer.
Bible: Offers assurance of salvation to all who are born again by the regeneration of the Holy Spirit.

"Hereby know we that we dwell in him, and he in us, because he hath given us of his Spirit" (1 John 4:13).

"And he that keepeth his commandments dwelleth in him, and he in him. And hereby we know that he abideth in us, by the Spirit which he hath given us" (1 John 3:24).

"But ye are not in the flesh, but in the Spirit, if so be that the Spirit of God dwell in you. Now if any man have not the Spirit of Christ, he is none of his" (Romans 8:9).

Easy Believeism: Instructs its hearers to make a decision (an act of the will) for Christ.

Bible: The Bible tells us to BELIEVE, and makes it clear that we are NOT born again by the will of the flesh or the will of man. To say that there is NO decision in salvation would be completely wrong, but to suggest that our decision saves us is equally wrong. We cannot of our will (decision) bring ourselves to new life. It is a miraculous spiritual regeneration which comes at the point of true belief (faith). Our only decision is whether we are willing to repent and hear the words of life that bring faith to us. Faith cometh by hearing, not by deciding.

"Which were born, not of blood, nor of the will of the flesh, nor of the will of man, but of God" (John 1:12-13).

"The wind bloweth where it listeth, and thou hearest the sound thereof, but canst not tell whence it cometh, and whither it goeth: so is every one that is born of the Spirit" (John 3:8).

"So then faith cometh by hearing, and hearing by the word of God" (Romans 10:17).

Easy Believeism: Claims that salvation is as easy as ABC or 123- just say this simple prayer.

Bible: The Bible says to STRIVE to enter in at the strait gate of salvation and that many will desire to enter and NOT be able. This does not mean work for salvation, but that the way of salvation is specific-repentance and faith. Anyone lacking either of which cannot enter in.

"Then said one unto him, Lord, are there few that be saved? And he said unto them, Strive to enter in at the strait gate: for many, I say unto you, will seek to enter in, and shall not be able" (Luke 13:23-24).

Easy Believeism: "Seals the deal" with a prayer.

Bible: True believers are sealed with the Holy Spirit.

> "In whom ye also trusted, after that ye heard the word of truth, the gospel of your salvation: in whom also after that ye believed, ye were sealed with that Holy Spirit of promise" (Ephesians 1:13).

> "Now he which stablisheth us with you in Christ, and hath anointed us, is God; Who hath also sealed us, and given the earnest of the Spirit in our hearts" (2 Corinthians 1:21-22.)

Easy Believeism: Demands a sinner's prayer as evidence of decision for Christ.

Bible: Commands those who believe to be baptized in the name of Christ. Throughout the New Testament, baptism was the first public profession of following the Lord Jesus Christ.

> "Then Peter said unto them, Repent, and be baptized every one of you in the name of Jesus Christ for the remission of sins, and ye shall receive the gift of the Holy Ghost" (Acts 2:38).

No matter how much we might want to deny it, we must face the truth that we have simply embraced "another gospel". We have loved the instant gratification and rewards of Easy Believeism/Prayerism, more than we have loved the truth. We have loved ourselves more than God. We have abandoned the word of God and embraced instead- that which is right in our own eyes. It is time for true Believers to stand up and proclaim the true gospel of Christ. We cannot continue to pretend that we do not see the truth.

> "But I fear, lest by any means, as the serpent beguiled Eve through his subtilty, so your minds should be corrupted from the simplicity that is in Christ. For if he that cometh preacheth another Jesus, whom we have not preached, or if ye receive another spirit, which ye have not received, or another gospel, which ye have not accepted, ye might well bear with him" (2 Corinthians 11:3-4).

Sadly, I know that most will continue to embrace the false in spite of the truth and simply turn a deaf ear to all warnings. Although I would not dare to guess anyone's motives, I can say without a doubt that the flesh is definitely fed with the illusion of results from Easy Believeism.

New Christians especially are enticed by such simple methods, and enthralled with the exaggerated reports. The accolades of such reports fuel a hunger for more and more. The excitement and comradery are hard to beat with biblical arguments or even logic. We boast of our inflated soul-winning numbers for the accolades of the congregation knowing full-well that the majority of professions were insincere at best. Shame on us! How could we take the blessed and glorious news of the gospel of Jesus Christ and minimize it to a mere numbers game?

Forgive me for saying this, but how utterly devilish it would be for a anyone to see the truth and choose for their own reasons to ignore it. Conversely, how unbelievably sad that so many would be so ignorant of the word of God or deceived about the way of salvation that they would not even see the truth. Practicing Easy Believeism is at best, ignorance and at worst, sinister.

Whether you're a teacher or a Mother, it's time to take responsibility for what we're teaching. We need to guard our kids against such potentially harmful practices. We must repent of our Easy Believeism gospel and return to preaching the biblical gospel of Jesus Christ.

CHAPTER 4
THE NOT-SO-OLD PATHS

Easy Believeism has been so widely accepted within Christianity that amazingly enough, today its methods are viewed as the *old paths*. Some of the greatest promoters of this heresy are now considered heroes of the faith. Many hold to the teachings of these old-time Evangelists as the solid fundamentals of the faith and resist all suggestions to the contrary. How utterly heartbreaking that the traditions of men should be held in such regard while the holy scriptures themselves should be rejected.

In the 1730's and 1740's, the Great Awakening began sweeping across Europe as well as North America. Preachers such as George Whitefield, and Jonathan Edwards were used greatly during this time to bring many to a saving knowledge of Christ. Relying on powerful sermon messages, they emphasized repentance and faith, and the evidences of a changed life which come from genuine conversion. They brought to light, through spiritual conviction, the personal need for an individual salvation in Jesus Christ. Johnathan Edwards' sermon: "Sinners in the Hands of an Angry God", is considered even today, one of the greatest sermons ever preached.

Even though a great number were saved through the preaching of these men, they never gave an altar call. In fact, an altar call was unheard of at that time. Instead of calling for a physical act of the will, they simply invited sinners to repent and come to Christ by faith. Although, they were known to have made themselves available to anxious sinners who desired counsel after their meetings, none were counseled to pray a prayer or to perform any other act in order to be saved.

This practice of counseling anxious sinners, eventually developed into what was known as the mourner's bench. Those who appeared to be visibly struggling under the conviction of the Holy Spirit were called forward to a mourner's bench where an attempt was made to counsel them during the service. Although the mourner's bench did not gain much ground initially, it did lay the foundation for our modern invitation system (altar call).

In the 1800's Charles Grandison Finney known as the "Father of the altar call" revived the mourners bench, bringing it to new heights of popularity. Finney's emphasis however, was quite different from that of his predecessors. He focused instead on stirring the emotions and manipulating the will in order to secure decisions rather than relying on the conviction of the Holy Spirit.

Finney believed that salvation is simply a matter of the will; thus, any means should be encouraged to convince sinners to agree to salvation. (Finney also denied original sin as well as the doctrine of imputation.)

Finney claimed that man is not saved, *not* because he *cannot* as the Calvinists suggest, but because he *will not*. While Calvinism certainly does err in claiming that there is no decision in salvation (as well as in many other areas), suggesting that our decision saves us is equally wrong. Repentance is a matter of the will, but salvation is not. We cannot of our will (decision) bring ourselves to new life. It is a miraculous spiritual regeneration which comes at the point of true belief (faith).

The very idea that a decision or mental assent is the catalyst for regeneration is a foundational error in the understanding of salvation. To reduce the regeneration of the Holy Spirit to an act of man's will is a great distortion of the very salvation we claim. No man has ever been born again by his own will, but only through faith in Jesus Christ. Our only decision is whether we are willing to repent and hear the words of life that bring faith to us. Faith cometh by hearing, not by deciding.

This error however, became the foundation of a monumental turning point for a widespread change toward decisional regeneration. The aim of Evangelism became selling the sinner on the idea of *accepting* salvation, rather than calling him to repent toward God and come to faith in Christ.

Soon, not only the anxious bench (as it was now called), but many other forms of physical and emotional manipulation were being accepted as valid methods of Evangelism. These new methods stirred the excitement of many, drawing huge crowds and making converts by the droves.

Although multitudes of *decisions* were made for Christ; it seemed that most were not being regenerated. Those who worked closely with Finney, questioned even then, the validity of these means when they saw great rates of these converts fall away.

One of Finney's many critics was John Williamson Nevin, who disagreed with not only the use of the mourner's bench but with many aspects of these *new measures* as they were called.

In *The Anxious Bench*, Nevin, almost prophetically warned of consequences that no man can measure arising from these *new measures*, setting us on a path that would lead to not only fanaticism, but laziness in the pulpit as well as superficiality in the pews. He rightly described the progression of these fanatical influences as a desolating flood. Once the gate had been opened for these methods, it seemed there was no stopping it.

Nevin's call to examination of these new measures was met with disproportionate opposition. Those holding to these practices were wildly antagonistic and attacking. Nevin recognized that because these practices were tied to the current revivals, many viewed them with an almost sacred nature, refusing to question their validity according to Bible standards. Much like today, any opposing such practices were vilified.

No amount of biblical truth could overcome the emotionalism incited by this babel of extravagance, as he called it. Preaching of repentance and faith, and then trusting in the power of the Holy Spirit to work within sinners' hearts was no longer enough. Men soon demanded to see instant results from their labors and were set to obtain them by any means.

A once solemn assembly turned into a riotous affair and the pulpit became a stage complete with theatrics and comedy. The spiritual was replaced by the emotional. Belief was replaced by a decision of the will and signified by a physical response, and so it is today.

Super salesmen Evangelists such as Billy Sunday, Billy Graham and more recently, Jack Hyles perfected the art of coercion and helped to set the standard for the Easy Believeism practiced today.

Just as a misunderstanding of the purpose of the will in salvation is at the heart of these *new measures*, so it is with our modern Easy Believeism gospel.

The use and purpose of man's will regarding salvation is exactly where most stumble. It is the classic point of tension between Calvinism and Arminianism. Decisional regeneration is simply Arminian error with a new twist. That is why the few who are willing to see the errors of Easy Believeism, often slingshot to the opposite and equally dangerous error of Calvinism.

Seeing these two philosophies as the only options for salvation, they begin to consider Calvinism & Lordship Salvation as possible alternatives and allow these false teachings to also be brought in to their Churches.

They reason that if it is not our decision that saves us, it must be God's sovereign will that determines who will and will not be saved, to the exclusion of any human responsibility whatsoever. They begin to accept the idea that some are simply predestinated to be saved while some are predestinated for Hell. Both Calvinism and Arminianism are extreme distortions of the gospel of Jesus Christ

"As if a man did flee from a lion, and a bear met him; or went into the house, and leaned his hand on the wall, and a serpent bit him" (Amos 5:19).

Somewhere between the two extremes of Calvinism and Arminianism lies a mediate position based on Biblical truth. When we look at the issue through the fog of our own positional preconceptions & pre-assigned definitions, it can be difficult to see that truth. We must compare scripture with scripture & find the truth that is consistent with God's character & his word.

The Five Points of Calvinism are generally set forth in the form of an acrostic on the word TULIP, as follows:

T-Total Depravity according to Calvinism's definition, means not only is man completely corrupted by sin as the Bible teaches, but is also because of his depravity, unable to do that which the Lord commands- to repent or believe.

U-Unconditional Election means that if man is unable to save himself because of the fall, and if God alone can save, and if all men are not saved, then the logical conclusion is that God has not chosen to save all men.

L-Limited Atonement means that Christ died to save a set number of sinners; that is, those chosen only.

I-Irresistible Calling means that when the Holy Spirit calls a man by His grace, that call is irresistible, that no man can refuse salvation.

P-Perseverance of the Saints means that those whom God has elected and effectually called and sanctified by His Spirit, can never totally fall from grace, but will be eternally saved.

The Five Points of Arminianism are, generally speaking, as follows:

1. Free will, or human ability. This means that man, although affected by the fall, is not totally incapable of choosing to do good, and is able to both repent and exercise faith in God in order to receive the gospel and to bring himself into possession of salvation.

2. Conditional election. This means that God called those individuals who, He knew or foresaw would believe and receive the gospel. God elected those that He saw would choose to be saved of their own free will and in their natural fallen state.

3. Universal redemption. This means that Christ died to save all men; but only in a potential way. Christ's death allowed God to pardon sinners, but only on the condition that they believed.

4. The work of the Holy Spirit to save is limited by the human will. This teaches that the Holy Spirit, as he begins to work to bring a person to Christ, can be resisted and His purposes frustrated. He cannot bring new life unless the sinner is willing to receive this life.

5. Falling from grace. This teaches that a saved man could fall from salvation. It is the logical and natural outcome of the system. If man can decide by his will to receive salvation, he can also will to refuse or return this gift.

Not all Calvinists believe every point of TULIP philosophy. There are many different types of Calvinists Hyper or 5 Pointers, Extreme, Moderate, three pointers…etc. Most Calvinists assume that anyone who is not a Calvinist must be an Arminian.

Calvinism focuses to one extreme on its understanding of God's sovereignty and our perceived inability, while Arminianism goes to the opposite extreme placing undo emphasis on man's responsibility and participation in salvation.

Arminianism's over-emphasis on man's will, attributes to it the responsibility for obtaining, as well as holding onto salvation. It teaches that since a man *decides* to be saved, then the logical conclusion would be that he can also *decide* later to be unsaved, and lose his salvation.

Although most Fundamental Bible believers today reject the latter, as well as the title of Arminian, they unknowingly embrace the former.

Decisional regeneration, which has paved the way for Easy-Believeism, is simply a poor imitation and extension of Arminian error- the opposite extreme of the Calvinist error.

Arminianism/Decisional Regeneration

Modern evangelism offers its message of Easy Believeism- the ABC's and 123's of salvation, making salvation as easy as *deciding to accept Christ*. Any who are willing to make a decision for salvation are promised entrance into Heaven in return for a simple prayer. Believe it or not, I have even heard it preached that anything more than a simple *decision* for salvation is heresy, and that any teaching of a struggle of faith is heresy as well. But what does the Bible say?

"Strive to enter in at the strait gate: for many, I say unto you, will seek to enter in, and shall not be able" (Luke 13:24).

The Bible tells us to strive, or struggle to enter into salvation, and that many will not be able. What does it mean to strive? It means to exert much effort or energy, to endeavor, to struggle or fight forcefully.

I heard a message once about striving to enter in at the strait gate. The Preacher explained that although many do desire to enter through the strait gate, they are not able to. Why? Not because salvation is difficult, or requires works, but because they are trying to squeeze through this narrow gate clutching their sin in one hand and their self-righteousness in the other. They simply cannot fit through that way. (Man must first be stripped naked of his own self-righteousness and be willing to let go of his sin.)

Sadly, though they cannot enter the strait gate holding onto their sin and self- righteousness, there are many standing outside the wide gate that will gladly usher them through there, offering them a false salvation. This broad, Easy Believeism way is plenty wide enough for them to fit through with all their baggage. Instead of being stripped of these things in humble repentance, they are assured that as long as they *decide* that they want salvation and profess that desire through prayer, they are indeed saved.

Entering through the strait gate is not as *Easy* as a simple decision, as they suggest. Only through repentance toward God and faith toward Jesus Christ are any able to enter in. Simply deciding that you want salvation is not enough. There must be both repentance and faith!

> "Enter ye in at the strait gate: for wide is the gate, and broad is the way, that leadeth to destruction, and many there be which go in thereat: Because strait is the gate, and narrow is the way, which leadeth unto life, and few there be that find it" (Matthew 7:13-14).

So often I hear preachers exhorting the unsaved to *get saved today*. "Now is the day of salvation…" (2 Corinthians 6:2), is misquoted and misused as a means of encouraging a quick response. "Today is the day of salvation" is proclaimed.

They tell the unsaved, "don't wait, do it today, there may not be another chance." They present it as though it were just another work, or item on someone's bucket list, as though being saved is something we can do ourselves. They give the impression that our decision is the catalyst for regeneration rather than faith.

To tell an unsaved man that he needs to be saved and that he should repent and believe are important truths, but to tell him to get himself saved implies that he has power over his own rebirth. It is telling him to do that which he cannot do. Speaking of rebirth, the gospel of John tells us "The wind bloweth where it listeth, and thou hearest the sound thereof, but canst not tell whence it cometh, and whither it goeth: so is every one that is born of the Spirit" (John 3:8).

We are not saved by our decision (our will). The Bible makes it clear that we are "born, not of blood, nor of the will of the flesh, nor of the will of man, but of God" (John 1:13).

As much as we may want to decide the moment of salvation, or manipulate it, it is simply beyond our control and our understanding. When we repent and believe on the Lord Jesus Christ, God saves us by the washing and regeneration of the Holy Spirit.

Giving an unsaved man any mechanical work to do regarding salvation is no less heresy than the blatant works-based salvation of any other false religion. Telling a self-sufficient humanist that he has the power, to be saved by his decision only feeds his allusion of self-rule. Giving a Roman Catholic a prayer to pray to be saved is no different than the prayers he prays as a means of penance.

Nowhere in the Bible are we told to decide to be saved, or to pray in order to be saved. I believe this is why we have so many people calling themselves Christians who may not be. These sincere people have been told that if they *really meant* what they said (their decision), then they can rest assured that they are saved, when in reality, this was simply the start of their conviction & a decision to repent.

In some cases, it is simply a beginning curiosity prematurely harvested. They are rushed into making a decision before repentance is even considered. There is no anguish of heart, no change of mind or turning to God from sin. Then we wonder why nothing changes in them. These people often show no fruit, no changed lives, & no desire to know the Lord, because their one little glimmer of conviction was mistaken for and labeled regeneration.

Some even attempt to equate repentance *with* salvation. They believe that because they one day decided to repent of their sin, that that was the day they decided to be saved. Some become discouraged & walk away; while others consider the prayer they said to be fire insurance or a get out of hell free card.

Others truly mark the day of their decision as the day they got saved and continue to seek the Lord. They go to Church & hear the word. Because of their repentant heart they are now willing to hear the words of life that minister faith to them. For a time, they aren't aware of much change in themselves, occasionally doubt their salvation, yet they cling to that day of decision as the day of their rebirth.

Then, sometime months or years later, something genuinely changes in them. They suddenly become aware of the Holy Spirit within them. The lights finally come on. They can now see & understand truths that were not revealed to them before. Their desires change; they are suddenly empowered by the Holy Spirit in areas of ministry or service. There must be an explanation for this. Charismatics might refer to this as the Baptism of the Spirit. Others may refer to it as receiving assurance of their salvation or their recommitment to Christ.

Might this actually be the day of their rebirth? The Bible describes salvation as coming to the knowledge of the truth. If the lights had not come on until now, were they not still blind and in the dark? Could they truly claim to have been saved if the eyes of their understanding had not been enlightened?

"For what man knoweth the things of a man, save the spirit of man which is in him? even so the things of God knoweth no man, but the Spirit of God. Now we have received, not the spirit of the world, but the spirit which is of God; that we might know the things that are freely given to us of God" (1 Corinthians 2:11&12).

Could they have become quickened and brought to newness of life and become new creatures and yet still be in the dark? Can the Holy Spirit of God come into anyone and bring them from a state of death to life and not create a noticeable change? Can the Holy Spirit fail to witness of itself or perform the duties of His office?

" Therefore if any man be in Christ, he is a new creature: old things are passed away; behold, all things are become new" (2 Corinthians 5:17).

If *any* man be in Christ, he is a new creature- not just some. Can a man be truly saved and *not* become a new creature? Not according to the word of God!

Some would say, "Well how can that be? I asked Jesus into my heart years ago. The Bible says that 'Whosoever shall call upon the Name of the Lord shall be saved', so that means I got saved the day that I called upon the name of the Lord."

Again, it is not our decision or our will that saves us. Our decision is only one of repentance & turning to God in order to receive salvation. Salvation is a spiritual work totally of God.

Our decision is evidence of our repentance and in some instances evidence of saving faith, but not in all cases. We are saved by grace through faith, not through our will, or decision. Not everyone who calls upon the name of the Lord does so in genuine faith in our Savior. Jesus made that clear: "Not every one that saith unto me, Lord, Lord, shall enter into the kingdom of heaven" (Matthew 7:21).

There must be true belief within the heart in order for that profession to be real. A profession without faith is worthless, not magical. To confess with thy mouth the Lord Jesus means to testify of the belief that you already have.

We cannot of our will (decision) bring ourselves to new life. It is a miraculous spiritual regeneration which comes at the point of true belief (faith). Our only decision is whether we are willing to hear the words of life that bring faith to us.

Faith cometh by hearing, not by deciding.

Salvation is NOT a matter of the will, but repentance IS. We do not *decide* to be saved. We decide to repent and become willing to hear the word of God which ministers faith to us. Deciding to be saved is NOT the same as repentance toward God and faith toward our Lord and Savior Jesus Christ.

So, what then is the message of the Bible? The Bible, tells us that we are condemned by our sins, and except we repent and trust in the Savior we will perish. It tells us God's plan for saving us and the means by which we can be saved. It tells us that we are saved by grace through faith, and we are commanded to repent and believe.

Nowhere does the Bible tell an unsaved man to decide, or to do anything else at all in order to secure his salvation. It does not tell him to walk an aisle, or say a prayer, or even to take care of that matter today. The only decision we have to make is whether we will repent; and we know that we are not saved by repentance, but by faith.

The biblical command then for the unsaved is simply to repent and believe. Repentance is the first command, for without repentance there is NO salvation. The Bible tells us that "God resisteth the proud, but giveth grace unto the humble" (James 4:6), and that "salvation is far from the wicked: for they seek not thy statutes" (Psalms 119:155).

Many have believed in God and even the facts of salvation and *not* been born again, because they had no repentance. Simply believing that there is a God is not enough, for even the demons believe and tremble.

When we turn from our wicked rebellion toward God, (repent) and become *willing* to hear the words of life found in the holy scriptures, faith cometh by that hearing and we are then made wise unto the *means* of salvation described within; "...how that Christ died for our sins according to the scriptures; And that he was buried, and that he rose again the third day according to the scriptures" (1 Corinthians 15:3) and "that whosoever believeth in him should not perish, but have eternal life." (John 3:15)

If we are exhorting the unsaved to trust in their "decision" (their will) that which does not save, it is no less than a false gospel we are preaching. Many people have made sincere "decisions" without repentance, or without true faith and were never truly born again. What they really meant one day, may be the farthest from their desires the next. Our emotions and very often our decisions are ruled by our fickle hearts.

53

"The heart is deceitful above all things, and desperately wicked: who can know it?" (Jeremiah 17:9).

The message of salvation is far too important and has been so confused and twisted by so many. We as the Church ought to at least be willing to use biblical terminology.

"For I am not ashamed of the gospel of Christ: for it is the power of God unto salvation to every one that believeth" (Romans 1:16).

Calvinism / Predestination

When I was a new Christian reading my Bible, I immediately came upon scriptures dealing with election, and predestination. "Wow. There it is," I thought. For a short time, I leaned toward Calvinistic thinking, entertaining the idea that God chose some for salvation while he also chose the rest for damnation.

It wasn't long though, before I saw that man's free will and God's command for him to repent and believe were also clearly spelled out. This *seeming* contradiction was difficult to handle, especially considering the extreme positions traditionally associated with each, which at their core, each demand the rejection of the other. Knowing that God's word cannot be wrong, I studied and prayed in an attempt to reconcile the two. I prayed to God that he would give me an understanding of truth that would reconcile the whole truth of his word.

"If any of you lack wisdom, let him ask of God, that giveth to all men liberally, and upbraideth not; and it shall be given him" (James 1:5).

God is good and true to his word! In time, he brought me to a place through the study of his word (the book of Ephesians in particular), where I could in my own limited understanding, reconcile each position with the other. I would not dare claim to have a perfect or even complete understanding of these difficult issues, but one that I believe is of God and harmonizes the scriptures beautifully, without contradiction. This, it seems is also not a *new* understanding, as I have since read others who claim this same belief. I pray that sharing this understanding will help someone else who may be struggling with these same tensions and possibly considering one or the other of these two extreme errors.

I simply cannot within this short book, sufficiently address all of the points of Calvinism, but I believe that if we could simply understand this key point, the rest of Calvinism's complicated and extensive philosophies will simply fall apart. I pray that some would grab on to this truth, if only for protection against the snare of Calvinism.

At its simplest form, it is this: That God predestinated the people and events that he would use to accomplish his greater purpose- to bring salvation to the entire world. All of predestination revolves around God's greater purpose which is shown throughout the entire Bible.

This may seem at first, to overly simplify such a seemingly complex theological issue, but I would ask you to please attempt, as far you are able, to prayerfully understand this position before rejecting it. I believe that if you do, you will see how that it can be applied without contradiction to every area of tension between the 2 positions and harmonize scriptures that are thought to be in conflict.

While predestination is a biblical term, the definition of this term is highly debatable. Predestination, according to Calvinism means that only some individuals are decreed by God to receive eternal life; which would demand the obvious (while often ignored) conclusion that some are excluded. Arminianism (the opposite error) states that those whom God foreknew *would choose* salvation are predestinated to receive it.

Paul's letter to the Church at Ephesus shines some light on the true meaning and purpose of predestination. Looking at the big picture here, we see that Predestination has more to do with fulfilling God's purposes than simply with individual salvation; that God predestinated the people & events that would fulfill his plan of making salvation available to all.

Ephesians chapters 1-3 is the clearest illustration of this. Calvinists and Arminians alike love to claim verses 4-6 of chapter 1 as proof of their own personal, eternal predestination. A quick reading of these verses would seem to support their conclusion; but upon closer investigation, Paul's message reveals something more.

Ephesians 1: 1 "Paul, an apostle of Jesus Christ by the will of God, to the saints which are at Ephesus, and to the faithful in Christ Jesus:

2 Grace be to you, and peace, from God our Father, and from the Lord Jesus Christ.

3 Blessed be the God and Father of our Lord Jesus Christ, who hath blessed us with all spiritual blessings in heavenly places in Christ:

4 According as he hath chosen us in him before the foundation of the world, that we should be holy and without blame before him in love:

5 Having predestinated us unto the adoption of children by Jesus Christ to himself, according to the good pleasure of his will,

6 To the praise of the glory of his grace, wherein he hath made us accepted in the beloved.

7 In whom we have redemption through his blood, the forgiveness of sins, according to the riches of his grace;

8 Wherein he hath abounded toward us in all wisdom and

prudence;

9 Having made known unto us the mystery of his will, according to his good pleasure which he hath purposed in himself:

10 That in the dispensation of the fulness of times he might gather together in one all things in Christ, both which are in heaven, and which are on earth; even in him:

11 In whom also we have obtained an inheritance, being predestinated according to the purpose of him who worketh all things after the counsel of his own will:

12 That we should be to the praise of his glory, who first trusted in Christ."

While Paul addresses this epistle *to* the Church, implying that what he is initially speaking of refers to the Church as a whole; what he is addressing is two distinctly different groups of people that make up the Church. He discusses in detail, the history of each of these two groups.

As non-Jewish people it can be hard for us to see from any other perspective than from that of the Church. Although Paul was God's chosen apostle to the Gentiles, he was a Jew & understood & spoke to us from that perspective. At the time Paul was writing this letter, it was still a relatively new idea to accept that God was now offering salvation to the Gentiles. The Jews still considered themselves to be the elite, chosen people of God, while the Gentiles were trying to establish their place in the Church.

The purpose of his letter was to address the growing problem of division within the Church between Jewish & Gentile believers and more importantly, to reveal to them a mystery that until now was unknown. Paul refers to God's purpose, according to the good pleasure of his will. What is the mystery of God's purpose that Paul is referring to? It is summed up for us in verses 9&10. Paul explains that it was God's plan from eternity. Therefore, Paul insists on unity in the Church.

"Having made known unto us the mystery of his will, according to his good pleasure which he hath purposed in himself: That in the dispensation of the fulness of times he might gather together in one all things in Christ, both which are in heaven, and which are on earth; even in him" (Ephesians 1:9-10).

A careful look at the book of Ephesians shows Paul's illustration of this mystery and a shift of focus from one group of people to another, from Jews to Gentiles. Paul begins in verse 1"...to the saints which are at Ephesus, *and* to the faithful in Christ Jesus" (italics mine).

In verses 3-12 he details the position of the Jewish people who were *first* to be blessed through God's plan, as the privileged elect. If you mark in your Bible, I would challenge you to highlight every *us* and *we* in one color and then choose another color for *ye* to better illustrate the contrast.

3 ...who hath blessed *us*...

4 ...he hath chosen *us* in him before the foundation of the world, that *we* should be holy and without blame before him in love: ...

5 ...Having predestinated *us* unto the adoption...

6 ... hath made *us* accepted in the beloved...

7 "In whom *we* have redemption through his blood...

8 ...he hath abounded toward *us* ...

9 Having made known unto us the mystery of his will...

10 That in the dispensation of the fulness of times he might gather together in one all things in Christ, both which are in heaven, and which are on earth; even in him:

11 In whom also *we* have obtained an inheritance, being predestinated according to the purpose of him who worketh all things after the counsel of his own will:

12 That *we* should be to the praise of his glory, who first trusted in Christ" (italics mine).

*Verse 13 shows the shift of focus.

13 "In whom *ye* also trusted, after that *ye* heard the word of truth, the gospel of *your* salvation: in whom also after that *ye* believed, *ye* were sealed with that holy Spirit of promise" (italics mine).

The question that must be asked is, who are the *we* and *us*, and who are the *ye*? Reading on further, Chapter 2: 11-19 leaves no doubt. *Ye,* refers to the Gentiles, who were far off, strangers from the covenants, but now are made nigh by the blood of Christ.

11 "Wherefore remember, that *ye* being in time past Gentiles in the flesh, who are called Uncircumcision by that which is called the Circumcision in the flesh made by hands;

12 That at that time *ye* were without Christ, being aliens from the commonwealth of Israel, and strangers from the covenants of promise, having no hope, and without God in the world:

13 But now in Christ Jesus *ye* who sometimes were far off are made nigh by the blood of Christ.

14 For he is our peace, who hath made both one, and hath broken down the middle wall of partition between us;

15 Having abolished in his flesh the enmity, even the law of commandments contained in ordinances; for to make in himself of

twain one new man, so making peace;

16 And that he might reconcile both unto God in one body by the cross, having slain the enmity thereby:

17 And came and preached peace to *you* which were afar off, and to them that were nigh.

18 For through him we both have access by one Spirit unto the Father.

19 Now therefore *ye* are no more strangers and foreigners, but fellowcitizens *with* the saints, and of the household of God"(italics mine).

Here we see Paul expounding on the mystery he is revealing, that God has gathered together in one, all things in Christ. The Gentiles were now fellowcitizens *with* the saints.

Remember in chapter 1 that Paul begins in verse 1"...to the saints which are at Ephesus, *and* to the faithful in Christ Jesus"? This is where many are confused. They read the word "saints", and assume that this is speaking to everyone in the Church, both Jews and Gentiles alike.

Many read this chapter and assume that they themselves, as Gentile believers are predestinated from the foundation of the world. This is understandably confusing, as we as Christians are also referred to as Saints in other passages of scripture, but we must rely on the context for clarification.

Who are the saints? Comparing scripture with scripture, we can see that the saints Paul refers to are his Jewish Brethren. Paul tells us that the Gentiles have become fellow citizens and joint-heirs *with* them.

"Now therefore ye are no more strangers and foreigners, but fellowcitizens with the saints, and of the household of God" (Ephesians 2:19).

"That the Gentiles should be fellowheirs, and of the same body, and partakers of his promise in Christ by the gospel" (Ephesians 3:6).

When Paul refers to the saints in this passage, it is clear that he is speaking of Jewish saints, and when he uses the terms *us* and *we*, he is also speaking of his Jewish brethren. When he shifts to the use of *ye*, he is speaking of Gentiles. With that understanding, let's go back and read at Chapter 1 again.

Ephesians 1: 1 "Paul, an apostle of Jesus Christ by the will of God, to the saints [His Jewish Brethren] which are at Ephesus, and to the faithful [Gentiles] in Christ Jesus:

2 Grace be to you, and peace, from God our Father, and from the

Lord Jesus Christ.

3 Blessed be the God and Father of our Lord Jesus Christ, who hath blessed *us* [Jewish believers] with all spiritual blessings in heavenly places in Christ:

4 According as he hath chosen *us* [Jewish believers] in him before the foundation of the world, that *we* should be holy and without blame before him in love:

5 Having predestinated *us* [Jewish believers] unto the adoption of children by Jesus Christ to himself, according to the good pleasure of his will,

6 To the praise of the glory of his grace, wherein he hath made *us* accepted in the beloved."

7 In whom we have redemption through his blood, the forgiveness of sins, according to the riches of his grace;

8 Wherein he hath abounded toward *us* [Jewish believers] in all wisdom and prudence;

9 Having made known unto *us* [Jewish believers] the mystery of his will, according to his good pleasure which he hath purposed in himself:

10 That in the dispensation of the fulness of times he might gather together in one all things in Christ, both which are in heaven, and which are on earth; even in him:

11 In whom also *we* [Jewish believers] have obtained an inheritance, *being predestinated according to the purpose* of him who worketh all things after the counsel of his own will:

12 That *we* [Jewish believers] should be to the praise of his glory, who *first trusted* in Christ. (italics mine)

Paul says that *we* (speaking of his Jewish brethren) have obtained an inheritance, "*being predestinated* according to the *purpose* of him who worketh all things after the counsel of his own will" (Ephesians 1:.12)

Notice here it is clear that they, the Jewish believers, were predestinated as a nation according to God's purpose, NOT individually for salvation. He goes on to further clarify: "That we [Jewish believers] should be... who first trusted in Christ" -that the Jewish people were predestinated to be the first to receive the promise. This fact is clearly supported throughout scripture.

Jesus told his disciples in Luke 24:47 "that repentance and remission of sins should be preached in his name among all nations, *beginning* at Jerusalem" (italics mine).

Most people think of the great commission in this way, that we are to reach our Jerusalem first, then a little farther away and then farther still. I believe that they are missing the significance of Jesus' instructions. Until the temple was destroyed in 70 AD, the lost Jews were still worshipping according to their traditional methods with temple sacrifices & offerings, which can never take away sins. Jesus told the disciples to go to the Jews first with one last attempt to save those who would believe. After that, we find out that God's judgment is passed upon them in that they were blinded until the fullness of the Gentiles come in.

God is a righteous judge. Throughout the Old Testament, we see that He sent Prophets or messengers to witness against them and to warn them before his judgment was passed upon them.

Hebrews 10:28 tells us: "He that despised Moses' law died without mercy under two or three witnesses"

The disciples were to be these witnesses to the Jews first, then to the Samaritans and finally to the Gentiles. This is the mystery Paul reveals, showing how God broke down the wall of separation between the Jews and Gentiles and fulfillment of God's promise to Abraham, that through him all the world would be blessed. This is the reason for Jesus' instructions to begin at Jerusalem, then Samaria and finally the rest of the world.

"Be it known therefore unto you, that the salvation of God is sent unto the Gentiles, and that they will hear it" (Acts 28:28).

Chapter 2 of Ephesians shows the contrast of the lost estate of the Gentiles who were "strangers from the covenants of promise, having no hope, and without God in the world" (Eph.2:12), but who now have become the elect according to the foreknowledge of God. The foreknowledge referred to is that of God's eternal plan promised to Abraham. "And I will bless them that bless thee, and curse him that curseth thee: and in thee shall all families of the earth be blessed" (Genesis 12:3).

Ephesians 2:1 And *you* hath he quickened, who were dead in trespasses and sins;

2 Wherein in time past ye walked according to the course of this world, according to the prince of the power of the air, the spirit that now worketh in the children of disobedience:

3 Among whom also we all had our conversation in times past in the lusts of our flesh, fulfilling the desires of the flesh and of the mind; and were by nature the children of wrath, even as others.

4 But God, who is rich in mercy, for his great love wherewith he loved us,

5 Even when we were dead in sins, hath quickened us together with Christ, (by grace ye are saved;)

6 And hath raised us up together, and made us sit together in heavenly places in Christ Jesus:

7 That in the ages to come he might shew the exceeding riches of his grace in his kindness toward us through Christ Jesus.

8 For by grace are ye saved through faith; and that not of yourselves: it is the gift of God:

9 Not of works, lest any man should boast.

10 For we are his workmanship, created in Christ Jesus unto good works, which God hath before ordained that we should walk in them.

11 Wherefore remember, that *ye being in time past Gentiles* in the flesh, who are called Uncircumcision by that which is called the Circumcision in the flesh made by hands;

12 That at that time *ye were without Christ, being aliens from the commonwealth of Israel, and strangers from the covenants of promise, having no hope, and without God in the world"* (italics mine)

Looking again at Chapter 1 verse 5 we see that the group of people Paul refers to as predestinated unto adoption of children by Jesus Christ were his Jewish brethren. Verses 11 tells us that they obtained an inheritance, being predestinated according to God's purpose. We can see that the predestination he is discussing in this verse is clearly NOT referring to Gentile believers, (or even the personal salvation of Jewish believers individually) but describes the part the Jews had in fulfilling God's greater purpose.

Paul painfully describes the condition of the Gentiles before Christ.

"Wherefore remember, that ye being in time past Gentiles in the flesh, who are called Uncircumcision by that which is called the Circumcision in the flesh made by hands; That at that time ye were without Christ, being aliens from the commonwealth of Israel, and strangers from the covenants of promise, having no hope, and without God in the world" (Ephesians 2: 11-12).

It should be glaringly obvious that the people who are referred to as predestinated unto the adoption of children, who obtained an inheritance, being predestinated according to the purpose, are NOT the same people who were strangers from the covenants of promise, having no hope, and without God in the world:

But, praise God, now the promise is fulfilled which was spoken to Abraham, and the purpose of God's predestinating is revealed, that through him all nations would be blessed. God predestinated the people and events that he would use to accomplish his greater purpose, which was to bring salvation to the entire world. All of predestination revolves around God's greater "purpose".

Ephesians 2:13 "But now in Christ Jesus ye who sometimes were far off are made nigh by the blood of Christ."

Ephesians 2:19 "Now therefore ye are no more strangers and foreigners, but fellowcitizens with the saints, and of the household of God" (emphasis added).

Paul further reveals the mystery:

Ephesians 3:3 "How that by revelation he made known unto me *the mystery*; (as I wrote afore in few words,
4 Whereby, when ye read, ye may understand my knowledge in the mystery of Christ)
5 Which in other ages was not made known unto the sons of men, as it is now revealed unto his holy apostles and prophets by the Spirit;
6 That the Gentiles should be *fellowheirs*, and of the same body, and partakers of his promise in Christ by the gospel" (italics mine).

Through Christ the Gentiles now have *become* fellow-heirs who previously had no inheritance. Fulfilling the prophesy of Hosea 2:23 "And I will sow her unto me in the earth; and I will have mercy upon her that had not obtained mercy; and I will say to them which were not my people, Thou art my people; and they shall say, Thou art my God."

"Which in time past were not a people, but are now the people of God: which had not obtained mercy, but now have obtained mercy." (1 Peter 2:10)

We see the same thing conveyed in 1Peter chapters 1 & 2, (as well as many other passages). We see that Peter is writing to the Church. He refers to them as *"elect according to the foreknowledge of God the Father"* (italics mine). He goes on to praise God for their salvation.
What is the foreknowlegde of God? Is it that of individual salvation? No. Again, it is the fulfilling of God's greater purpose, which was to bring salvation to all. Those who were not a people are now, a people.

"Of which salvation the prophets have enquired and searched diligently, who prophesied of the grace that should come unto you" (1 Peter 1)

He tells them that the Prophets spoke of this salvation that would come to them. Why? He further goes on to clarify:
"But ye are a chosen generation, a royal priesthood, an holy nation, a peculiar people; that ye should shew forth the praises of him who hath

called you out of darkness into his marvelous light. Which in time past were not a people, but are now the people of God: which had not obtained mercy, but now have obtained mercy" (1Peter 2: 9 & 10).

He understood this mystery that they are now the elect according what the prophets proclaimed was God's plan to bring salvation to the entire world.

The beautiful simplicity of this truth shines in stark contrast to the complicated, and often illogical teachings that are necessary to support both the Arminian and the Calvinist position. Often elaborate assumptions and hairsplitting doctrines are necessary to explain away the natural understanding of scripture, in order to make either work in light of the other.

If we could only grasp this truth, it would allow us to see that a biblical understanding of Predestination in no way prevents anyone from being saved, neither does it exclude our human responsibility, or our free will.

What is our responsibility? To repent. Paul preached: "Testifying both to the Jews, and also to the Greeks, repentance toward God, and faith toward our Lord Jesus Christ" (Acts 20:21).

We've made predestination much more complicated than it should be. If we could simply read the scriptures without filtering everything through or presuppositions and what we've been taught; and step back to look at the bigger picture of God's plan for the world instead of just our own personal salvation, we might see the simplicity of his plan.

Lordship salvation

The evidence of true salvation is shown by our surrender to Christ's authority and in a changed life.

"Therefore if any man be in Christ, he is a new creature: old things are passed away; behold, all things are become new" (2 Corinthians 5:17).

While it is good that we are beginning to recognize that Easy Believeism has oversimplified the gospel message to the point of making it basically a magic prayer, many have also erred by attempting instead, to add extra demands, in an attempt to "de-simplify it". This has resulted in the trend toward Lordship Salvation. The reasoning is this: "If we make sure these people *really, really* mean the prayer that they say, or make a *real* commitment to Christ, surrendering to his authority, then surely they will be truly saved.

Making Jesus Lord is not a condition of salvation, but a result. Many people today insist that in order to be saved, we must make Jesus our Lord. But, consider this question: Can a man serve two masters? Can a servant simply choose another Lord or master? Before we are saved, we as lost men and women are in bondage to our sin, powerless to break away. As slaves to that sin, we are servants to obey it.

"Know ye not, that to whom ye yield yourselves servants to obey, his servants ye are to whom ye obey; whether of sin unto death, or of obedience unto righteousness?" (Romans 6:16.)

"No servant can serve two masters: for either he will hate the one, and love the other; or else he will hold to the one, and despise the other" (Luke 16:13).

Before we are saved, we do not have the freedom or the power to choose another Lord or Master, because we are slaves to our sin. But when we see our sinful desperate condition as a lost sinner condemned to Hell and turn in faith to Jesus as our Savior, we are purchased by His blood. We are bought with a price, and sealed with the Holy Spirit" the earnest of our inheritance" (Ephesians1:14).

We then are no longer slaves to sin as children of the Devil, but are freed from the bondage to sin and become instead sons of God. Although Jesus has been and always will be Lord of all; by his purchase He becomes our rightful owner and our personal Lord as well as our Savior. We then become his willing servants of righteousness.

"But God be thanked, that ye were the servants of sin, but ye have obeyed from the heart that form of doctrine which was delivered you.18 Being then made free from sin, ye became the servants of righteousness" (Romans 6:17).

Now as servants of righteousness, doing the Father's will, the mind and purpose of Christ, becomes our mind and purpose as well. Jesus' Lordship over our lives is evidence of our salvation, evidence of our freedom from our bondage to sin, not the cause. If you are saved, and Jesus still is not your Lord, having rule and reign over your life, or if you are still in bondage as a servant of sin, then it might be an indication that you have not truly been saved yet.

When we recognize our sinful condition and condemnation before God and turn to Christ our Savior for rescue, we believe in him and are saved. The one who redeems our soul becomes our Lord. We are saved because we believe in what he has done already on our behalf, dying on the cross to pay for our sins and rising again to bring us newness of life. We are not saved because we decide to commit to him and make him Lord. Salvation is all in what He has done, not in what we do. We cannot decide, or even surrender our will to him to be saved. We can only believe in what he has done. Remember, our repentance is toward God, our holy creator who we have sinned against, and our faith is in Christ, the one who came to save us. Trying to will ourselves to make him Lord is NOT the same as believing in him for salvation.

"But though we, or an angel from heaven, preach any other gospel unto you than that which we have preached unto you, let him be accursed" (Galatians 1:8).

We do not need more man-made philosophies to try to manipulate regeneration. What we need is to simply return to biblical preaching with biblical terminology and trust God to do as he says he will do. Paul preached "...repentance toward God, and faith toward our Lord Jesus Christ" (Acts 20:21).

When asked, "What must I do to be saved?", his answer was not, "Make Jesus Lord of your life." It was simply, "Believe on the Lord Jesus Christ, and thou shalt be saved" (Acts 16:31).

The answer isn't to add to or change the gospel of Christ, but to simply preach the true gospel of Christ in Biblical terms.

"And they went out, and preached that men should repent" (Mark 6:12).

"He that believeth on him is not condemned: but he that believeth not is condemned already, because he hath not believed in the name of the only begotten Son of God" (John 3:18).

"For by grace are ye saved through faith; and that not of yourselves: it is the gift of God: Not of works, lest any man should boast" (Ephesians 2:8-9).

Adding these requirements for salvation, or even as a means of keeping salvation is no less than adding works to the gospel message.

CHAPTER 5
THE COMMISSION TO EVANGELIZE CHILDREN

If you were to ask any Christian today about their Church, you would undoubtedly get an enthusiastic response describing their thriving Children's ministries and youth groups. Some of the more elite Churches even boast a Christian school on the premises. But if you asked these same people about the soul-winning or discipleship programs at their Church their eyes would glaze over and a confused look would quickly spread across their faces.

We spend countless hours, and enormous amounts of money on clubs, classes and bus ministries sincerely trying to reach children for Christ, but is this really what God would have us do?

Decisional regeneration and a lust for numbers is partly responsible for the recent turning to child evangelism as the primary outreach of the Church today.

If salvation is as easy as coercing a decision and a prayer, then who is easier to coerce than a child?

Children are easily manipulated and will often do anything we ask if it means they will receive praise for it. It sure is more fun, rewarding and a lot less intimidating to witness to children. They do not offer intellectual arguments or challenge our beliefs. Most times they are simply so eager to please that they will agree to anything we suggest, especially if their friends are doing it as well.

Often, those who are not biblically grounded or equipped to share the gospel, having not studied to show themselves approved unto God, are too afraid and intimidated to witness to adults. They fear that their ignorance will cause them shame and discredit their testimony. But these same people are quite comfortable sharing their immature and often unbiblical gospel message of Easy Believeism with children (and we allow it). Shame on us!

We can recruit just about anyone that professes to be a Christian to work in children's ministries, but ask these same people to go soul-winning or to witness to adults and they run for the hills. New Christians, and sometimes even the unsaved are allowed to work in children's ministries. Then we have the nerve to claim that getting children saved is the most important thing to us? If it were as important as we claim, wouldn't it also be important to know well, and be sound in our doctrine before teaching these little ones? Could it be that it is not really as important to us, as it is Easy?

Let me state very clearly that I am NOT suggesting that we discontinue children's ministries altogether. I emphatically agree that we should train up children in the way in which they should go, raising them in the nurture and admonition of the Lord. I believe in Christian education as well. The question that must be asked however, is this:

Should Child Evangelism really be the primary emphasis of the Church?

Somehow, we have allowed children's ministries to become the primary focus of the modern-day Church. "What's the problem with that?" you might ask. The problem is that this was not the focus of the early Church, nor is it what we are commanded to be doing.

In the early Church, the men had great responsibilities to learn. They continued daily, steadfastly in the apostles' doctrine. Then, not only did they teach their own wives and children the things of God at home, but they were also responsible to preach to and to teach other men as well so that they in turn, could do the same – that is, teach their wives and children as well as others.

"And the things that thou hast heard of me among many witnesses, the same commit thou to faithful men, who shall be able to teach others also" (2 Timothy 2:2).

Where are these "faithful men" who are "able to teach others also?" and why are they letting the women run the Church? Whether we want to admit it or not, even within Fundamental Bible believing Churches, where a firm stand is taken on the Bible teaching that only men are qualified to fulfill the roles of Pastors, Deacons, and teachers of men, women are still running the Church.

As women, we are born nurturers and have a natural desire to serve the ones we love. Because of this, it is common to see more women involved in serving than men. Since a woman's heart is always more tender toward the children and since women are, according to the Bible, not to teach men nor usurp authority over them, their focus is generally toward children.

In recent years, Children's ministries have grown to such numbers that they dwarf all other ministries within the Church. Often, they become so large that the men are also brought in to help. As a matter of fact, in many Churches today, the majority of Church ministries are now geared toward children and very few, if any directed toward the evangelization or discipleship of adults. So now, the few men that do serve are devoting all their time and energies to the children's ministries as well. And many of these are unable or unwilling to teach.

68

Now, I'm not suggesting that it is wrong for men to teach children, as a matter of fact, it is biblical for the fathers to teach their own children to love and serve the Lord. I also believe that there is nothing wrong with corporately teaching our children the things of the Lord and planting seeds of faith so that they might one day be saved. However, we have gotten so far from what the Bible teaches, that now the women, in their leanings toward children have, basically taken over the Church and convinced us that child evangelism is the Biblical priority.

I know that this is hard for many to see and to accept, but surely if this was to be our priority as the Church, then God's word would have given us clear instructions on it. The Apostles were not running camps and games and face-painting for the children, they were preaching to and teaching adults. The biblical pattern for the Church is this:

"But I would have you know, that the head of every man is Christ; and the head of the woman is the man; and the head of Christ is God" (1Corinthians 11:3).

Christ over the man and man over the woman. Ladies, the God-given responsibilities and commands to the men should take priority over our desires toward children's ministries.

"And in those days, when the number of the disciples was multiplied, there arose a murmuring of the Grecians against the Hebrews, because their widows were neglected in the daily ministration. Then the twelve called the multitude of the disciples unto them, and said, It is not reason that we should leave the word of God, and serve tables. Wherefore, brethren, look ye out among you seven *men* of honest report, full of the Holy Ghost and wisdom, whom we may appoint over this business. But we will give ourselves continually to prayer, and to the ministry of the word. (Acts 6:1-4 italics mine)

"And he said, *Men, brethren, and fathers*, hearken; The God of glory appeared unto our father Abraham, when he was in Mesopotamia, before he dwelt in Charran" (Acts 7:2).

"*Men and brethren*, children of the stock of Abraham, and whosoever among you feareth God, to you is the word of this salvation sent" (Acts 13:26).

"Be it known unto you therefore, *men and brethren*, that through this man is preached unto you the forgiveness of sins" (Acts 13:38).
"And when there had been much disputing, Peter rose up, and said

unto them, *Men and brethren*, ye know how that a good while ago God made choice among us, that the Gentiles by my mouth should hear the word of the gospel, and believe" (Acts 15:7).

"And when the town clerk had appeased the people, he said, Ye *men* of Ephesus, what man is there that knoweth not how that the city of the Ephesians is a worshipper of the great goddess Diana, and of the image which fell down from Jupiter?" (Acts 19:35).

Every man knows that if he doesn't do something, there is a woman standing close by that is eager to prove herself and take on his work. He then cleverly turns his responsibilities over to his unwary companion and rests happily upon his laurels. Who wouldn't? Umm…women. This is nothing new. Deborah was an example.

Deborah was NOT a positive example of God's call for women to lead the Church, but a judgment on the failure of the men that God had called to lead Israel into battle.

"And Deborah, a prophetess, the wife of Lapidoth, she judged Israel at that time. And she dwelt under the palm tree of Deborah between Ramah and Bethel in mount Ephraim: and the children of Israel came up to her for judgment. And she sent and called Barak the son of Abinoam out of Kedeshnaphtali, and said unto him, Hath not the LORD God of Israel commanded, saying, Go and draw toward mount Tabor, and take with thee ten thousand men of the children of Naphtali and of the children of Zebulun? And I will draw unto thee to the river Kishon Sisera, the captain of Jabin's army, with his chariots and his multitude; and I will deliver him into thine hand. And Barak said unto her, If thou wilt go with me, then I will go: but if thou wilt not go with me, then I will not go. And she said, I will surely go with thee: notwithstanding the journey that thou takest shall not be for thine honour; for the LORD shall sell Sisera into the hand of a woman. And Deborah arose, and went with Barak to Kedesh" (Judges 4:4-9).

Deborah was indeed, a judge in the Old Testament that God used in a mighty way, but God did not call her to lead Barak into battle, but simply to rebuke him for his disobedience and lack of faith. When Deborah called Barak, and spoke to him, notice that it wasn't with a new message from the Lord. Barak was already very aware of God's instructions. Deborah simply reminded him of something he apparently knew. Look at vs. 6 "…and said unto him, Hath not the LORD God of Israel commanded, saying, Go and draw toward mount Tabor, and take with thee ten thousand men of the children of Naphtali and of the children of Zebulun?"

Deborah was rebuking him for his disobedience to the Lord. She asked him, "Didn't God command you to go?" He knew that God had called him to lead Israel into battle, but for some reason, was delaying or resisting. It becomes clear as we read that the reason was a lack of faith and possibly fear. He told Deborah that he would only go if she went with him. We read that she did go with him into battle, but this was not what God desired, it was a judgment and a shame on Barak.

Look again at vs. 9 "And she said, I will surely go with thee: notwithstanding the journey that thou takest shall not be for thine honour; for the LORD shall sell Sisera into the hand of a woman."

Deborah told him that because of his failure, he would not receive the glory for this victory, it would go to a woman instead. This was a great shame and humiliation to him, and a just punishment for his cowardice and lack of faith.

I guess it is true as Solomon said, that "there is nothing new under the sun." Today, just as in Old Testament times, men because of fear or lack of faith, fail to lead and willingly give the glory that God intended for them, to women. It is still just as great a failure, and shame on them, as it was on Barak.

If there is a choice between going out and preaching the word to adults, or staying in to play with the kids, is it any wonder most people choose to stay? This does not however excuse our failure to do that which God has called us to do, simply because we have come up with another plan. Our great God who cannot lie and does not change, will never go against his own word! He has made it clear that men are to train other godly men who shall be able to teach others as well (and that includes their own families).

Even within solid Churches like my own, where there is no shortage of knowledgeable Christian men, well prepared to teach others, often their time and energies are consumed instead by children's ministries. This can be seen with the many godly women as well. Those who could be soul-winners and used of God to lead other women to the Lord and disciple them, have spent every ounce of energy and every spare moment they have preparing games and snacks and lessons for the children instead.

If the entire Church was not already engrossed in children's ministries, they just might be more interested in soul-winning, and discipling believers. Ladies, it's time we stepped back and started encouraging our husbands to do what God has commanded them to do, instead of offering our own ideas as a substitute! If we were encouraging saved, godly men to truly fulfil their God-given responsibilities, I sincerely doubt that they would have time to play games in the gym and pass out candy.

Ask yourself this question: If children's and youth ministries were not an option, what would *you* be doing to share the gospel? Would it burn within you until you found someone to share it with? (If not, then there's already a problem). Would you write letters, visit nursing homes, prisons, or maybe even your neighbors with the message of Christ? Would you go out into the parks or grocery stores and maybe even festivals handing out tracts and sharing the gospel with any that would listen? Isn't that what we should be doing now?

Some claim that we must reach people *through* their children.

Many sincere philosophies have been developed to justify our actions. I have heard many say, "If it weren't for the kids' programs, the parents wouldn't come." Why not? Obviously, it is because they are not saved themselves. If the parents were saved, they would come.

I've heard Missionaries many times tell of how they begin first by setting up children's ministries. They go in with balloon animals, face-painting and children's games to win the parents' trust. The problem is that these are merely the philosophies of men and not the biblical commands of God

Why have we done this? Because we have failed to go and preach the gospel to the parents. We have not fulfilled our responsibility to preach the word, and make disciples, so naturally the people are not saved and not training up their own children in the nurture and admonition of the Lord. Rather than try to cure the disease, we attempt to treat the symptoms. The Church now attempts to assume the responsibility of training up every child in town.

Instead of fulfilling our responsibilities to the adults of the community, we decide that we will become a surrogate parent of sorts, training up all the children in town. We go out and gather them all up once a week, teach them things that are contrary to what they learn at home, and hope that they will witness to their parents and possibly lead them to Church. Then we use award ceremonies, plays and all sorts of worldly enticements to bring the parents in. Even in the rare cases where we do manage to get a parent in, the end simply does not justify the means if the means are not biblical.

We cannot claim to be true Bible believers and measure our methods by these scant results. If that were a valid determination, then we would have to also accept the methods of the Mega Churches and thriving false religions as equally valid. We must determine the true worth by how closely it adheres to the scriptures. The word of God is the ONLY true test. All doctrine and spiritual understanding must be established by scripture.

What we are doing is trying to put the cart before the horse. Just imagine if we went out and reached the parents, and the parents were truly saved and discipled. These parents would then raise their own children in the nurture and admonition of the Lord, and be able to go out into the world and be witnesses, making disciples as well.

Why are we so afraid to go out and witness to adults? Because, not only is the Church full of false converts, but even those who are saved are not strong in the word. Most Christians today have not been discipled or equipped to even witness.

"And the things that thou hast heard of me among many witnesses, the same commit thou to faithful men, who shall be able to teach others also" (2 Timothy 2:2).

If child evangelism was truly intended to be the primary avenue to spread the gospel, wouldn't there be biblical examples for us to follow? Where are the stories of the Apostles seeking after the children of Jerusalem or Samaria or the Utter-most parts of the earth? Where are the stories of children being baptized after Peter preached at VBS or AWANA? Where are the commands to teach faithful children, that shall be able to teach their parents also?

Do we honestly believe that God somehow failed to foresee the need today to reach families through their children? Could we even suggest that God's instructions to us were incomplete? Or have we just become wiser than God?

There are no written accounts of children being evangelized or saved in the scriptures. Instead, what we see is Jesus and the Disciples focusing their efforts on adults. Why? Because they were commanded to teach faithful men who would be able to teach others also.

The disciples and the early Church were obediently following the commands of God, (and not the women) teaching faithful men who would be able to teach others also. Somehow, we have abandoned the biblical patterns set forth in the scriptures and begun to go a different direction. We have decided that we know better than God. Instead of going out to preach, and making disciples of those who are saved, we stay in and play games with the kids. Child Evangelism cannot take the place of what God has commanded the Church to do.

When did we decide that we would place children's ministries over the commandments of God? Or are we just too afraid to hold the men to the standard that God demands? Ladies, it's time to allow the men to take the lead once again! If we would follow the biblical pattern set forth in the word of God, maybe we would have faithful men and women to train up their own children to love the Lord.

I realize that this is a sacred cow to many, and some of you reading this are already offended. Many genuinely godly Christians have spent years devoted to ministering to children. Please do not misunderstand; I am not in any way suggesting that it was without value! It is vitally important to teach children the things of God, but it must be God's way and in his timing.

These unbiblical philosophies of children's ministries however, illustrate our distorted perception of the purpose of the Church. The Church is a called-out assembly of believers. The Church as the body of Christ, is to function together as a whole, fitting together perfectly to accomplish the task of fulfilling the Great Commission. It is a filling and equipping station for disciples of Christ, preparing them and teaching them the things they need to know to go and do the same. Somehow, we have lost sight of that image of the Church.

"Go ye therefore, and teach all nations, baptizing them in the name of the Father, and of the Son, and of the Holy Ghost: Teaching them to observe all things whatsoever I have commanded you..." (Matthew 28:19-20).

The Great Commission is basically this: We are to go and preach. Then the saved are baptized and join themselves to the Church, where they are then taught to go and do the same. Preach, baptize, teach, preach, baptize, teach...etc.

Child Evangelism Cannot fulfil the Great Commission

As much as we want to believe that Child Evangelism is our greatest priority, this just simply does not line up with what God has commanded us to do.

Some would suggest that they are following God's command, evangelizing and then discipling these children; but is that really what we're doing? If so, why are they NOT bearing fruit? Why are they NOT evangelizing and making disciples of their own?

Instead of bringing in buses of children, we should be sending out buses full of well equipped, soul-winners, prepared to make disciples!

Child Evangelism simply cannot fulfil the great commission, because:

1. Very few of these children are even really saved.
2. Those who are saved, are often too young and lacking in biblical wisdom and discernment to share the message with others and in turn disciple them, making new disciples and carrying on the pattern set forth.

Very few if any of the children we evangelize are really saved. Even some who might be saved, are too young and lacking in biblical or even natural wisdom and discernment to share the message with others and in turn disciple them, carrying on the pattern set forth.

If these children are not truly saved, how successful can our discipleship really be? We know that the unsaved cannot understand spiritual things.

"But the natural man receiveth not the things of the Spirit of God: for they are foolishness unto him: neither can he know them, because they are spiritually discerned" (1 Corinthians 2:14).

As we have already seen, most of our children's ministries produce false converts through Easy Believeism, or at best become a lengthy salvation process. Biblical evangelism in the early Church was not committed to focusing on the same people for ten or fifteen years, (that was called parenting). Bringing up a child in the nurture and admonition of the Lord is the job of the father, not the Church.

"And, ye fathers, provoke not your children to wrath: but bring them up in the nurture and admonition of the Lord" (Ephesians 6:4).

The Disciples went out and preached the word. Those that were saved were joined to the Church to be taught and trained to continue the work. Those who refused were not entertained and cajoled for years. When the word was not received, the disciples were to brush the dust off their feet and continue on to the next place. Now, that is not to say that they did not earnestly plead and present their case to whomever they had opportunity.

They did not spend years trying to reach the same people over and over. For the sake of obedience, they went out further and further to proclaim the message to others, focusing their time and attention teaching those who did believe. The believing who were discipled were then equipped to go out and win souls, making more disciples. That is the basic principle of growth.

"And the word of God increased; and the number of the disciples multiplied in Jerusalem greatly; and a great company of the priests were obedient to the faith" (Acts 6:7).

"Therefore they that were scattered abroad went everywhere preaching the word" (Acts 8: 4).

Instead of going out and making more disciples, the majority of converts from our Child evangelism eventually turn from God. We commit ten to fifteen years, getting these kids *saved* and *discipling* them only to see them walk away.

75

Generally, the only ones who do continue to seek God as adults are the ones who were raised in the Church by godly Christian parents, and even those are not able to evangelize and teach others until they are adults. Even then, we know that a great percentage of even these children leave at the first opportunity. Our methods are just NOT working.

The Great commission is more than simply making converts and even baptizing them. We are commanded to teach them all things that Jesus commanded (to make disciples).

Discipleship today has become nothing more than training others to lead children's ministries. We need to redefine evangelism and discipleship. Disciples are those who are committed to following Christ.

We must see that corporate evangelism of children can never come close to fulfilling the great commission. How can this be the pattern that God described in his word? If this is not what God would have us to do, then we are in disobedience, no matter how we might feel about it.

Are we even commanded to *evangelize* children?

To some, this question might seem like a *no-brainer*. But the answer might surprise you. The Bible tells us to: "train up a child in the way in which he should go: and when he is old he will not depart from it." (Proverbs 22:6)

This verse however, was not a command for the Church, but a command for the parents to teach their own children at home. It was written before the local Church even existed. This verse is also a command for a much more in depth training than simply leading children through prayers and pronouncing them saved.

While we *are* commanded to evangelize the *lost*, there is no evidence that the disciples or the early Church interpreted that as a command to specifically focus our efforts on *child evangelism*. (Obviously children would hear the word of God along with their parents within the Church, but the primary emphasis of the Church's evangelism was not children as it is today.)

We are commanded to *biblically educate* our children, teaching them God's laws and his word and instilling in them a fear of the Lord that will lead them to repentance and faith. Of course, all of our Bible teaching should point to Christ and to the good news of the gospel (the evangel); but our aim should not be to simply secure professions from children to the neglecting of adults.

Matthew 18:1-14 is viewed by many as the *commission* to evangelize children; but looking at this passage in its proper context reveals a much different meaning.

Matthew 18:1 "At the same time came the disciples unto Jesus, saying, Who is the greatest in the kingdom of heaven?

2 And Jesus called a little child unto him, and set him in the midst of them,

3 And said, Verily I say unto you, Except ye be converted, and become as little children, ye shall not enter into the kingdom of heaven.

4 Whosoever therefore shall humble himself as this little child, the same is greatest in the kingdom of heaven.

5 And whoso shall receive one such little child in my name receiveth me."

A superficial reading of these verses apart from the rest of the chapter might seem to support view. Many like to look at verses 1-14 alone, and verses 15 on as a different topic altogether, (that of Church discipline) but they cannot be divorced from each other, because we see in verse 15 the word moreover which makes it clear that this is a continuation, or clarification of this same issue. Without acknowledging this very important point, many confuse what Christ is saying. The issue discussed from the beginning throughout the end of the chapter is the same. Viewing the chapter in its entirety as well as the parallel passage in Mark brings it all together perfectly.

The Disciples were arguing over who was greatest in the kingdom, obviously, each hoping to earn that title. A lesson on humility and true service is what Jesus is teaching them.

Who is the greatest? It is not who you might think. Not the wisest or the strongest, but the least. Jesus calls a child to come and illustrate this point. As teachers, we love object lessons. We love to use an everyday physical object to illustrate a spiritual truth. This is exactly what Christ is doing. He shows them a helpless, trusting child with seemingly nothing to offer to the kingdom of Heaven, but only needy and wanting.

He tells them in verse 3 that unless they become like this, they cannot even enter the kingdom of Heaven. Then, he presents the kicker. Not only is salvation received that way, through humility and helplessness, completely trusting in God's grace, but greatness is also measured that same way.

"Whosoever therefore shall humble himself as this little child, the same is greatest in the kingdom of heaven" (Matthew 18:4).

The person who humbles himself like a child is the greatest in the kingdom of Heaven. He is showing them that their thinking on greatness is completely wrong. The one who appears to be least is the greatest.

When we are saved, we are born again as babes in Christ, helpless and completely dependent upon the Savior for life. We even drink the milk of the word to help us grow until we are able to eat the meat.

"And whoso shall receive one such little child in my name receiveth me" (Matthew 18:5).

Whoso receives one such little child- who is it referring to when it says one such little child? Obviously, it is the same person it was speaking of in verse 4, the one who humbles himself becoming as a child- this babe in Christ. Those who receive us, patiently guiding us and teaching us, help us along our way. Christ says that when we do this, receive such a one, it's as if we are doing these things for him personally.

However, if we should offend such a one, it is a great and terrible offense to him personally. The word offend means to cause them to stumble. How do we cause a seeker or a new Christian to stumble? Through sin, false doctrine, unloving attitudes, we can hinder their growth and even prevent them from coming to salvation.

"But whoso shall offend one of these little ones which believe in me, it were better for him that a millstone were hanged about his neck, and that he were drowned in the depth of the sea. Woe unto the world because of offences! for it must needs be that offences come; but woe to that man by whom the offence cometh! Wherefore if thy hand or thy foot offend thee, cut them off, and cast them from thee: it is better for thee to enter into life halt or maimed, rather than having two hands or two feet to be cast into everlasting fire. And if thine eye offend thee, pluck it out, and cast it from thee: it is better for thee to enter into life with one eye, rather than having two eyes to be cast into hell fire. Take heed that ye despise not one of these little ones; for I say unto you, That in heaven their angels do always behold the face of my Father which is in heaven" (Matthew 18:6-10).

Many would argue that one of these little ones could literally be a child, and not simply a babe in Christ. How can we know for sure? The parallel passage in Mark gives us a bit more information than is recorded here. For, whatever reason, Matthew, by the inspiration of the Holy Spirit chose to leave this part of the conversation out of his account. Mark's account makes it clear that this is indeed speaking of the babe in Christ, who as a child, is considered least.

"Whosoever shall receive one of such children in my name, receiveth me: and whosoever shall receive me, receiveth not me, but him that sent me. And John answered him, saying, Master, we saw one casting out devils in thy name, and he followeth not us: and we forbad him, because he followeth not us. But Jesus said, Forbid him not: for there is no man which shall do a miracle in my name, that can lightly speak evil of me. For he that is not against us is on our part. For whosoever shall give you a cup of water to drink in my name, because ye belong to Christ, verily I say unto you, he shall not lose his reward. And whosoever shall offend one of these little ones that believe in me, it is better for him that a millstone were hanged about his neck, and he were cast into the sea" (Mark 9:37-42).

We see Christ speaking of any man, even the least who does service in the name of Christ, is doing it as unto him and should not be offended. The warning is given to those who would cause such "little Children" in the faith to stumble through sin or false doctrine or even discouragement.

Therefore, he continues, if your hand offends you or causes you to sin in a way that would cause these to stumble, cut it off. If your foot causes you to sin, cut it off as well.

Returning to Matthew 18:15, he continues to address even the occasion that these babes in Christ might sin against us, and how we are to deal with them.

"Moreover if thy brother shall trespass against thee, go and tell him his fault between thee and him alone: if he shall hear thee, thou hast gained thy brother. But if he will not hear thee, then take with thee one or two more, that in the mouth of two or three witnesses every word may be established. And if he shall neglect to hear them, tell it unto the Church: but if he neglect to hear the Church, let him be unto thee as an heathen man and a publican" (Matthew 18:15-17).

Matthew 19:14 is also frequently cited as a command to evangelize children: "But Jesus said, Suffer little children, and forbid them not, to come unto me: for such is the kingdom of Heaven."

Now, obviously, if Christ had, as many insist, already established child evangelism in chapter 18, why would these disciples be forbidding these children to come? It is obvious that was not the case.

Another important point to consider in the passage is that Jesus told his disciples not to forbid the children from coming to him; but what were they coming to him for? Their parents brought them to Jesus so that he would lay hands on them. It was an act of blessing, not a matter of salvation. As a matter of fact, when we look at the parallel passage in Luke, these children are described as infants. Does an infant have sufficient understanding to believe unto salvation? Certainly not.

"And they brought unto him also infants, that he would touch them: but when his disciples saw it, they rebuked them" (Luke 18:15).

We are not told that these infants were saved, or baptized or anything else, so why would we construct such an assumption that Christ has commanded us to evangelize children? It is never even implied that we are to seek after children to evangelize, but simply that we are not to prevent them from hearing of and being drawn to the Savior.

Here is another verse which is also claimed as justification for our emphasis on child evangelism:

"Verily I say unto you, Whosoever shall not receive the kingdom of God as a little child shall in no wise enter therein" (Luke 18:17).

This again, is illustrating the childlike humility necessary for salvation, however; some take this verse to the extreme, suggesting that if we don't get people saved as children, they will not be saved at all. That is quite a stretch of the true meaning. This of course, does not mean that, but simply that they must receive him with child-like faith.

Neither of these verses, when viewed in their proper context can stand as a biblical precedent for child evangelism. If Jesus, or the disciples interpreted them that way, it certainly would have been a great and urgent matter in *every* generation to evangelize children. We should expect then to have seen at least some of the disciples practicing child evangelism, and yet we don't. Surely, there would have been some pattern set forth for the Church for such.

There are in fact, NO scriptures that tell us to focus our evangelism efforts on children and no examples of the disciples or the early Church doing so. Children's ministries such as we practice today did not come into existence until the early twentieth century. The over-emphasis on children's ministries is the result of our own desires and human reasoning.

Child Evangelism as our primary outreach may seem right in our own eyes; but what if God knows better than us? What if there are reasons he has not commanded us to focus our efforts on evangelizing children? Will we trust him and obey?

CHAPTER 6
AGE OF ACCOUNTABILITY

Ever since I became a Christian I have heard people refer to the mysterious doctrine of *the Age of Accountability*. It is spoken of as an indeterminate age when a child is able to clearly understand and thus become accountable to God for their own actions and/or beliefs (making them accountable for their sin). Those who are not yet mature enough to clearly understand are considered under the age of accountability. Because there are no clear scriptures specifying a set age, we can only speculate based upon an individual's intellectual, emotional and spiritual maturity.

With our lack of understanding of this issue comes much confusion as to when and how children should be evangelized. Modern Christianity spends thousands upon thousands of dollars every year, not simply teaching our own children the fear of the Lord, as commanded in scripture, but in an attempt make them understand and become accountable for their sin at the earliest possible age. Not only that, but we round up every child we can find, bring them in, quickly offer them as much information as we can (in between snacks and games of course) and then we hold them accountable as well.

-But what if God is not yet holding them accountable? How would this change our evangelism?

-If we weren't focusing all our efforts on evangelizing children, who would we then be focusing on? Adults maybe?

-Would we still be pushing nursery and elementary children to ask Jesus into their hearts?

Shouldn't we at least make an honest attempt to search the scriptures to find a biblical basis for our practices? While there are a few scriptures that do suggest an age of accountability, such as David's response to the death of his child, we do not have a clear answer as to what age that is.

"But now he is dead, wherefore should I fast? can I bring him back again? I shall go to him, but he shall not return to me" (2 Samuel 12:23).

The Bible does not tell us how old David's child was, but David was obviously confident that his child would go directly to be with the Lord.

"And should not I spare Nineveh, that great city, wherein are more than sixscore thousand persons that cannot discern between their right hand and their left hand; and also much cattle?" (Jonah 4:11).

81

In this verse the Lord states that there are 120,000 people who do not even know their right hand from their left. That is quite a statement. What sort of people would be so lacking in knowledge and understanding that they would not know their right hand from their left? Children possibly? It is not clear, but what is clear is that God desires to spare them and show them mercy because of their lack of discernment.

There appears to be no clear age specified in the Bible where God declares anyone old enough to be accountable for their sin. Or is there?

> "Moreover your little ones, which ye said should be a prey, and your children, which in that day had no knowledge between good and evil, they shall go in thither, and unto them will I give it, and they shall possess it" (Deuteronomy 1:39).

Again, we see God referring to those who cannot yet discern good and evil. In this very familiar account the children of Israel have sent men to spy out the land that God has promised them. Ten came back fearful and murmuring against God, not believing God would see them safely into the land. They feared for their wives and children and would not follow the Lords commands. Two however followed God wholly and gave report of the blessings awaiting them in the land.

The Lord told them that because of their unbelief, they would not enter into the promised land, but their children whom they did not trust God to protect, would. God would not hold these children accountable for the sin of unbelief, but all the rest of the people (the adults) would be held accountable. How old were the children that God said would not be held accountable? All that were under twenty years old. God calls them little ones.

> "Your carcasses shall fall in this wilderness; and all that were numbered of you, according to your whole number, from twenty years old and upward, which have murmured against me, Doubtless ye shall not come into the land, concerning which I sware to make you dwell therein, save Caleb the son of Jephunneh, and Joshua the son of Nun. But your little ones, which ye said should be a prey, them will I bring in, and they shall know the land which ye have despised. But as for you, your carcasses, they shall fall in this wilderness. And your children shall wander in the wilderness forty years, and bear your whoredoms, until your carcasses be wasted in the wilderness" (Numbers 14:29-33).

Wow! That is a very different age than the age *we* are attempting to make children accountable today. We see this event recounted again with the age of twenty being the determination of accountability in Numbers 32:11

82

"Surely none of the men that came up out of Egypt, from twenty years old and upward, shall see the land which I sware unto Abraham, unto Isaac, and unto Jacob; because they have not wholly followed me".

Twenty is also the age a man was counted in census and also able to go to war. "From twenty years old and upward, all that are able to go forth to war in Israel: thou and Aaron shall number them by their armies" (Numbers 1:3.)

It is even more interesting that at age twenty, the age when a man is now recognized as numbered among the people, he is also now required to offer tribute for his own soul.

"Every one that passeth among them that are numbered, from twenty years old and above, shall give an offering unto the LORD" (Exodus 30:14).

Jamieson, Fausset & Brown Bible commentary: This was not a voluntary contribution, but a ransom for the soul or lives of the people. It was required from all classes alike, and a refusal to pay implied a wilful exclusion from the privileges of the sanctuary, as well as exposure to divine judgments. (Commentary on Exodus 30 by Jamieson, Fausset & Brown 1871) See also: Matthew Henry's Commentary.

There is a definite link between understanding and accountability/imputation of sin.

So, does this prove that the age of accountability is twenty? No, of course not. It would be foolish to be so dogmatic. What it does prove however, is that there is most certainly a relationship between understanding and accountability.

If we are going to be biblical or even logical, we would certainly have to admit that there is at the very least, a definite possibility that the children we spend so much time and effort attempting to *get saved* are not even yet accountable to God (while we neglect the adults who are without question, accountable already).

Would we ever dare suggest that a four or five-year-old child who just *got saved* was, moments before their profession, condemned to an eternity in the fires of Hell? No. Of course not, because we know that Children, because of their lack of understanding, are not yet accountable for their sins.

If they are not old enough to be accountable and condemned for their sin, then what in the world do we think they are being saved from?

I personally would lean toward believing that a child is not accountable to God until they have reached the point where they are now no longer under the authority of the parents. Does this mean that I believe we should *wait* to teach them *about* salvation? NO! We should always be teaching them.

As long as they are under the authority of parents, God entrusts us with their teaching, correcting and chastening. Why? Because they are still learning. Just as they are not yet ready to vote, or drive, or marry, they do not yet know what they need to know to be responsible for themselves. Even our court systems recognize these things and do not hold children accountable for their actions, but often the parents instead if they fail to teach them properly.

I believe that once they have outgrown or removed themselves from their parents' authority, it is then that God begins to deal with them directly. Hopefully, by this time, they have learned the difference between good and evil and have come to a place of repentance and faith.

Where there is no understanding of good and evil, there is no accountability. You might suggest that even a small child can understand right and wrong. I have myself, even seen toddlers display what seems to be a knowledge of right and wrong when they lie or attempt to hide their wrongs for fear of punishment. This does not however prove that they know good or evil. A knowledge of good and evil is much more than simply knowing that they have been disobedient to their parents.

Who is good? Only God himself is good. An understanding of good and evil therefore is related to God himself. It is an understanding of our sin as an offense to God himself.

But what about original sin?

"Wherefore, as by one man sin entered into the world, and death by sin; and so death passed upon all men, for that all have sinned" (Romans 5:12).

Because of Adam's disobedience, everyone is born into the world, spiritually dead and physically progressing toward death, because we are all under the condemnation of sin. This is proven by the simple fact that as Adam, all die. Even babies die. So, if they die in sin, without being saved, what would make us think that they are able to be in the presence of God, when the rest of sinful creation cannot?

It is a matter of accountability, or imputation of sin. When we are saved, our sins are covered by the blood of Christ. Our sins are no longer imputed to our account, but Christ's righteousness instead. It is not that we no longer sin, but simply that our sin is no longer imputed to us. God views us as righteous and we are accepted by him because our account of sin has been settled.

"Saying, Blessed are they whose iniquities are forgiven, and whose sins are covered. Blessed is the man to whom the Lord will not impute sin" (Romans 4:7-8).

So, it is with children. Although they are born under the condemnation of sin and in their flesh, will eventually die; that sin is not imputed to their account. It is not held against them because of their lack of understanding. If they do not yet comprehend God's laws, they will not be judged by them and condemned. Because sin is not imputed to them, they can be viewed as righteous by God and accepted into Heaven with him.

"...for where no law is, there is no transgression" (Romans 4:15).

"(For until the law sin was in the world: but sin is not imputed when there is no law" (Romans 5:13).

What law is being referred to here? Is this speaking only of the law of Moses? If men were not accountable for their sin simply because they did not have access to or know of the law of Moses, this would certainly excuse a great many generations and nationalities. Comparing scripture with scripture, we can easily see that is not the case.
From the Garden, we see that God communicated his word to man and held him accountable for the knowledge that he had. God gave Adam and Eve one clear commandment. They understood what God expected and yet they disobeyed and were judged. Cain and Abel also understood what God desired from them.

"And Abel, he also brought of the firstlings of his flock and of the fat thereof. And the LORD had respect unto Abel and to his offering: But unto Cain and to his offering he had not respect. And Cain was very wroth, and his countenance fell. And the LORD said unto Cain, Why art thou wroth? and why is thy countenance fallen? If thou doest well, shalt thou not be accepted? and if thou doest not well, sin lieth at the door. And unto thee shall be his desire, and thou shalt rule over him" (Genesis 4:4 -7).

God's word tells us that even the Gentiles, which have not the law, are a law unto themselves.

"For when the Gentiles, which have not the law, do by nature the things contained in the law, these, having not the law, are a law unto themselves" (Romans 2:14).

Again, knowledge is key. It would seem reasonable then, that without a knowledge of sin, children are not accountable for their sin and able to go directly to Heaven when they die. This very special relationship with God is illustrated in the following passage of scripture. God says that these are his children.

"Moreover thou hast taken thy sons and thy daughters, whom thou hast borne unto me, and these hast thou sacrificed unto them to be devoured. Is this of thy whoredoms a small matter, That thou hast slain *my* children, and delivered them to cause them to pass through the fire for them?" (Ezekiel 16:21, italics mine).

We may not be offering these children as sacrifice to other gods, but if we are giving them a false salvation that ultimately leads to their destruction, then we might as well be. These precious souls that belong to God, have been entrusted to us as a great privilege to raise them up for him. It is our job to represent our heavenly Father to them. As we teach them to love and obey us, we are preparing them to one day love and obey their Heavenly Father as well. We have been given these children by God, to raise them up, not for ourselves, but for him and for his glory alone. To fail to do so is no small matter.

While they are young, we instruct them and guide them and even chasten them as needed. Although they belong to God, we are the primary authority in their lives. We are a physical representation of God's authority to teach them how to obey him. They answer to us and we are responsible for them until the time that they answer to God for themselves. Just as we read in Galatians, an heir answers to tutors and governors until the time appointed of the Father. While we know that in this passage, these tutors and governors of course are a picture of the law, preparing us for faith, there is another very important lesson we can learn.

"Now I say, That the heir, as long as he is a child, differeth nothing from a servant, though he be lord of all; But is under tutors and governors until the time appointed of the father" (Galatians 4:1-2).

That child, without proper training and maturity is simply not ready to accept the responsibility, or accountability that goes along with being an heir. Therefore, he is under the authority of teachers, and those who will help to prepare him for that great responsibility. What age might that be? We cannot know. Only the Father knows that, but until they do know good and evil, they are not ready to answer to God.

That is why God gives children parents and teachers. It is our job to ensure that they receive the best preparations humanly possible, so that they will be able to one day stand as a fitting representation of his heritage, strong enough to withstand the enemy.

If we sent our young child to these tutors and governors to be trained for such a time, and they sent him home the same day, claiming that he is already prepared to answer for himself and to assume his rightful place; we would be furious.

We would never want our child to be robbed of the important lessons, or experiences necessary to teach him the truths he will need, but that is exactly what we do the children that come through our children's ministries. We bring them in for a night, lead them through a prayer and then send them back to their parents, assuring them that their child is now prepared for eternity. How dare we?

Who do we think we are to make such decisions for others' children? How in the world do we believe that we can meet a child one time and even come close to accurately assessing their intellect, emotional maturity, or understanding of spiritual things? How insanely arrogant, and even worse, unloving! We can't even be sure of these things with our own children.

What we are doing is removing any possible conviction of sin and need for repentance they may have by assuring them that their salvation has already been secured. We are not planting good seed in their hearts but uprooting it, and replacing it with tares that will choke out any further seed that may be planted in the future.

Ladies, we (myself included) have shirked our God-given responsibilities to these children. Why in the world would we try to shortchange a child on the spiritual training God has commanded us to give them? Why would we even want to pronounce them accountable prematurely? -especially someone else's child? I would think that we would desire every single opportunity that God allows to prepare them to love and serve him and to teach them as much as we possibly can about his holiness and perfect standard of righteousness. Wouldn't we want every moment to teach them of repentance and faith before they are responsible to answer to him on their own?

Instead, we are in such a hurry make them accountable to God, that we give them a bare bones gospel and run them through a sinner's prayer. Then we breathe a big sigh of relief, and pat ourselves on the back as though our job is done. We should be ashamed!

We have not even come close to preparing these children for eternity. A simple mention of sin is often all we give. Most of the children we pronounce saved have no idea what sin is, other than an offense to Mom and Dad. They do not understand good and evil or that their actions are an offense to a holy and perfect God who demands our obedience. Without a correct understanding of their own sin and condemnation before God, they cannot even see their need for Christ as Savior. Often, they do not even have a correct understanding of who God is, or why they are separated from Him. The Bible tells us that:

"The fear of the LORD is the beginning of wisdom: a good understanding have all they that do his commandments: his praise endureth for ever" (Psalms 111:10).

In order to teach children the fear of the Lord, we must first teach them who God is, and what his righteous commands for us are.

Who is this God that he should be feared? God is holy, and good, merciful and compassionate. He knows all and sees all, and is everywhere all the time. He is terrible, all powerful, righteous and just in judgment. He is the God of the Old Testament. The same now as he ever was- he does not change. Only when they know who he is, can they truly revere him, and desire to be reconciled to him.

Through learning his laws, they begin to see his holiness in contrast of their own sin, and recognize their lost condition. And by learning of his righteous judgment of the wicked, they recognize his just judgment of their sin and need for a Savior. In seeing God's great mercy and provision, they see his great love for man and recognize his great grace and unspeakable gift.

"The fear of the LORD is the beginning of wisdom: and the knowledge of the holy is understanding" (Proverbs 9:10).

Today, many well-meaning Christians in an effort to lead little ones to the Lord are short-cutting to the edited Easy Believeism gospel instead, and short-changing these kids' spiritual education. We just want to hurry up and get them saved, then teach them. We want to reap before we sow. Children especially are lacking in the foundational beliefs necessary to prepare them for faith in Christ. What does God's word tell us we use to prepare children for faith in Christ? Is it the gospel? No- It is the law.

"And these words, which I command thee this day, shall be in thine heart: And thou shalt teach them diligently unto thy children, and shalt talk of them when thou sittest in thine house, and when thou walkest by the way, and when thou liest down, and when thou risest up.

And thou shalt bind them for a sign upon thine hand, and they shall be as frontlets between thine eyes. And thou shalt write them upon the posts of thy house, and on thy gates" (Deuteronomy 6:6-9).

Understanding the law of God, teaches us the difference between good and evil and shows us our need for a Savior. We are so anxious for them to be saved that we often neglect the very important place that the law has in leading us to faith.

"Wherefore the law was our schoolmaster to bring us unto Christ, that we might be justified by faith" (Galatians 3:24).

The apostle Paul also spoke of the effects of the law.

"For I was alive without the law once: but when the commandment came, sin revived, and I died. And the commandment, which was ordained to life, I found to be unto death. For sin, taking occasion by the commandment, deceived me, and by it slew me." (Romans 7:9-11)

Paul stated that he was alive once without the law, but when the law came, (when he understood) he died. The law as our school master is beautifully illustrated through the words of Paul.

Romans 7:7 "... *I had not known sin but by the law:* for I had not known lust, except the law had said, Thou shalt not covet." (italics mine) **[I did not recognize my sinful lust as covetousness until I knew the law]** (emphasis mine)
8 "But sin, taking occasion by the commandment, wrought in me all manner of concupiscence. For without the law *sin was dead.*" (italics mine) **[Without the law, it seemed that there was no condemnation of my sin, as though it was not sin at all.]** (emphasis mine)
9 For *I was alive* without the law once: but when the commandment came, sin revived and I died." (italics mine) **[Before I knew what sin was, I believed I was alive and well in God's sight, fully able to stand before him; but when the law to light the sinfulness of my sin, it condemned me instead.]** (emphasis mine)
10 And the commandment which was ordained to life, I found to be unto death. **[When I understood God's law, I was no longer alive in my innocence, but dead in sin]** (emphasis mine)
11 For sin, taking occasion by the commandment, deceived me and by it slew me.
12 Wherefore the law is holy, and the commandment holy, and

just, and good.

13 was then that which is good made death unto me? **[How can this thing which brought condemnation and death be good?]** (emphasis mine) sin that it might appear sin working death in me by that which is good; *that sin by the commandment might become exceeding sinful.* (italics mine) **[The goodness of the law taught me the evilness of sin]** (emphasis mine)

14 For we know that the law is spiritual: but I am carnal, sold under sin.

15 For that which I do I allow not: for what I would, that do I not; but what I hate, that do I. **[My own action, and inability to do good confirmed that the law is good while I am not, and brought me to repentance- a change of mind wherewith a rebellious sinner can now agree with the law and the judgment of God.]** (emphasis mine)

16 If then I do that which I would not, I consent unto the law that it is good."

The law is what we should be using to teach children the fear of the Lord and to bring them to faith in Christ. Yet we tell these children sometimes at three and four years old, to *just accept Jesus,* neglecting to teach them about God's laws and his standards- the very things that show them their need for Jesus. Why are we short changing our kids with an edited gospel and limiting their opportunity to learn the fear of the Lord? What we are doing with these children is shameful.

Moms and teachers, it is our job to take the time to teach them the fear of the Lord and to "bring them up in nurture and admonition of the Lord" (Eph. 6:4) so that they will understand their need to repent toward God. Only then will they be willing to hear the words of life that minister faith to them. It is only through faith that they can receive salvation, not through a decision. We should never tell anyone that they are saved. Only they themselves and God can know that with certainty.

Teachers are not called to be the sole mediators of salvation. It is not their job to pronounce them accountable, that is not even up to the parent, but up to the Father. Telling a child that they are saved is so much more of an offense than even to an adult.

A prayer without repentance and faith is worthless. This is illustrated in the parable of the sower:

"But he that received the seed into stony places, the same is he that heareth the word, and anon with joy receiveth it; Yet hath he not root in himself, but dureth for a while: for when tribulation or persecution ariseth because of the word, by and by he is offended. He also that received seed among the thorns is he that heareth the word;

and the care of this world, and the deceitfulness of riches, choke the word, and he becometh unfruitful. But he that received seed into the good ground is he that heareth the word, and understandeth it; which also beareth fruit, and bringeth forth, some an hundredfold, some sixty, some thirty" (Matthew 13:20-23).

Those who received the word with gladness *chose* to believe, but because of hardness of heart, (unrepentance) the seed of faith was unable to take root. Their choice obviously did nothing. We see that they only "dureth" for a while. That does not sound like eternal salvation to me. Now regarding today's children's ministries and Easy Believeism gospel, that decision would have been taken as faith and these led through a prayer and told they were saved. They quite simply would have been lied to.

Our ministries encourage children to make these same decisions for Christ, most often without even a mention of God's laws, or repentance toward God.

When the stony ground of their unrepentant heart is unable to allow the word of God to take root, that word that was heard simply withers and fades away, without producing faith. To say that we are doing them a great disservice is an understatement. Our ministries are just not working!

Does that mean we should not corporately teach children?

It certainly does NOT. What it means is that we should be teaching them what God has told us to teach them- the fear of the Lord through his laws, to prepare their hearts for the time when they will be ready for salvation.

Do we then withhold the gospel? Of course not! But our aim in teaching should not be securing professions, but successfully educating them in all of God's word. We should be preparing them with the knowledge of God, and of good and evil, as well as what repentance is and how to be reconciled to God. The Church can either be a support in this effort, or a great stumbling block.

When I was first saved, because of my own biblical ignorance, I relied entirely on the Church for my children's spiritual education. Now however, because of the serious dangers. many times my husband and I have agonized over the question of whether to allow our children to participate in the children's ministries which practice Easy Believeism.

I don't believe that withholding them is the answer either. To deprive them of relationships with godly Christians and the additional support they offer is certainly not ideal, not to mention the practical difficulties of attempting to keep them out of these clubs.

While excluding them is difficult, trying to correct the false teachings they learn in these activities is almost impossible without also diminishing respect for their authorities. We have chosen to keep them involved on a limited basis, and lovingly correct all misunderstandings and false teachings as they arise. We have at times, discussed our desires with their teachers, asking that we be the only ones who address our child's salvation. Although this can be a difficult request for the teachers who practice group evangelism, most teachers are very understanding and cooperative.

Occasionally our requests have been met with unfavorable responses. Questions such as, "Why don't you want your child to get saved?" are posed, revealing much confusion on the part of the teacher. These can either produce great opportunities to share the truth, or drive a big fat wedge between us and the teacher. Sadly, the latter is much more common.

Like most parents, we sincerely appreciate the time and effort that so many put into the teaching of our children and greatly desire their help, although we as parents should be their primary teachers.

Many who do not attend Church, send their children to these ministries and also rely solely upon the teachers for their children's spiritual upbringing. In this case, the Church can either be a tremendous support to the parents, or a great spiritual danger to the children. Often, this additional responsibility creates within the teachers an undue urgency to *get these kids saved* in the short time that they may be there.

Ideally, the Church should be willing to work together along-side the parent in educating these children, (and to also teach the parent if necessary) according to biblical truth, and trust God for the results.

CHAPTER 7
WITHOUT A LOVE OF THE TRUTH, IT'S ALL JUST RELIGION

Some might say, "So what, if child evangelism is not what God commanded us to be doing, some are still being saved. How can it be wrong?" Can I suggest that they are being saved *despite* our false gospel and faulty methods, not *because* of them? Just think how many more would come to true faith if we were preaching a biblical gospel and fulfilling the great commission according to *God's plan?*

Does it really matter? It certainly *does* matter to God how we do things. How can we possibly look into his word and think that it doesn't? Offhand I can think of several examples: Aaron's sons took it upon themselves to offer strange fire before God. What was God's response? He struck them dead.

"And there went out fire from the LORD, and devoured them, and they died before the LORD" (Leviticus 10:2).

"Uzza, reached out his hand to steady the ark, which was resting upon an unsteady ox cart, although he knew he was never to touch it. What was God's response? He was also struck dead. And the anger of the LORD was kindled against Uzza, and he smote him, because he put his hand to the ark: and there he died before God" (1 Chronicles 13:10).

Another example would be Saul. God commanded Saul to utterly destroy all of the Amalekites, men, women, infant and suckling, ox and sheep, camel and ass as well as all that they had. But Saul chose to do things his own way. He saved alive King Agag, and also the finest of the sheep and oxen.

"And Samuel came to Saul: and Saul said unto him, Blessed be thou of the LORD: I have performed the commandment of the LORD. And Samuel said, What meaneth then this bleating of the sheep in mine ears, and the lowing of the oxen which I hear?" (1 Samuel 15:13-14).

"And Samuel said unto Saul, I will not return with thee: for thou hast rejected the word of the LORD, and the LORD hath rejected thee from being king over Israel" (1 Samuel 15:26).

Not only have we rejected the word of the Lord, and chosen to do things our own way; but if we were honest, we would have to admit that the Church today isn't even full of bleating sheep, but goats instead. We no longer go out and preach to adults, but stay in and play with the kids, or go out and invite the unsaved in. Now we lure the unsaved into the Church, through our children's ministries, woo them, and entertain them, make them a part of things, and hope that they will eventually become saved.

If the body of Christ is now made up of unbelievers as well as believers, (the dead as well as the living) how healthy can it possibly be? The body of Christ, meant to function as one cohesive unit cannot do so if the members themselves are not healthy and strong. When one member suffers, all suffer. When one is weak and sickly, the whole body suffers. Is it any wonder the Church today is full of sin and wickedness and failing to thrive? We are not equipping the saints within our called out assembly, but entertaining the sinners.

Our unbiblical methods do not produce lasting fruit

"... And the Lord added to the Church daily such as should be saved" (Acts 2:47).

How we win them determines how we will keep them. In the early Church people were saved, and THEN they were added to the Church, where they were discipled and prepared to then go and share the word and teach others as well.

Instead, we now invite the unsaved to come and be a part of the Church in hopes that they will eventually become saved. Sometimes they do get saved that way, but much more often they simply become part of the "Church" without ever being saved.

To entice these unsaved people to join themselves with the Church, unbiblical methods are often employed. They are not drawn to Christ by the Holy Spirit through the word, but to the Church through the ways of man. Because "the natural man receiveth not the things of the Spirit of God: for they are foolishness unto him: neither can he know them, because they are spiritually discerned" (1 Corinthians 2:14).

We resort to fleshly appeals to draw them- music, entertainment, food, games, and ridiculous outreach extravaganzas. Serious problems arise from these new methods. The problem is that how we draw them, is generally how we will keep them. If they are here for the fleshly appeal they will be gone as soon as it is no longer appealing. Then we marvel that they went out from us.

But they were not of us; for if they had been of us, they would no doubt have continued with us: but they went out, that they might be made manifest that they were not all of us" (1 John 2:19).

The unsaved that do stick around are often put to work, to build their relationships and encourage their loyalty to the Church. They become more comfortable and less convicted as they convince themselves that they truly are part of the body.

We have done them as well as the true Church a great disservice when this happens, for we know that "they that are in the flesh cannot please God" but we are now helping them to convince themselves that they are. An unsaved person should not feel comfortable around the saved. For "what fellowship hath righteousness with unrighteousness?"(2 Corinthians 6:14).

Our responsibility to the unsaved is to lovingly evangelize and disciple them, encouraging them to turn from their sins to God and believe in Christ. Instead of being convicted as a carnal person, still in sin, surrounded by spiritual, they become very comfortable as we make every effort to convince them they *are* a part of the body.

However, since they are not saved, they do not understand spiritual things, and often do not agree with Christian standards. Sincere believers have a very different lifestyle. Their dress, speech, and their social interests should not be the same as an unsaved person's therefore saved people seem peculiar, and often become laughingstocks to them. It is natural for man in his carnal state to have an aversion to them.

Many times however, it is not the unbeliever who changes, but the Christian who ends up compromising his standards to accommodate the comforts of the unbeliever. If a Church full of believers is truly living for the Lord, then it will be an uncomfortable atmosphere for the unsaved. It should still be a loving and welcoming place where they can come and be ministered to, but if it is set apart, holy and sanctified unto the Lord, and preaching the truth of the word, it will not be comfortable to the carnal man.

The very fact that the unsaved *are* so comfortable in our Churches is not a testimony of our love, but an indictment against our lack of spirituality. Of course, they should be welcomed to come and hear the message of the gospel so that they might be saved, but often we welcome them into membership and pretend that they are saved, soothing any discomfort and removing any convictions they may be having

These unsaved Church goers are rarely interested in discipleship or evangelism, or godly living (having not been truly converted) leaving the functioning body of the Church in a sense crippled, having now parts that do not function as they should.

Our job as the Church is not to add members by any means we can; it is to lift up the Savior and proclaim his message of salvation to the world. We are "Ambassadors for Christ" as though God did beseech them by us… "be ye reconciled to God" (2 Corinthians 5:20).

"And I, if I be lifted up from the earth, will draw all men unto me" (John 12:32).

We are to preach the word, not trick people into hearing it with movies and fellowship dinners and Christian-ish activities. When believers are drawn to join themselves to a Church because they are saved and desire to unite themselves with other believers as part of the Church, not only will they be more likely to stay, and to grow but to also raise their own children to serve as healthy members of the body.

Our youth groups are a prime example of our unbiblical practices.

The Church, as the body always has a great responsibility to lead others to Christ, but HOW we do that is vitally important. This may be hard for many to hear and is in no way meant to be hurtful or to drive away any unsaved teens or adults. It is a message intended for discerning Christian Moms who desire to be obedient to God and to protect their children from the world.

As Christians, we do everything we can to protect our kids and separate from bad influences. In many Churches, we even keep the boys and girls separated from each other during the elementary years, but then when they are adolescents, with raging hormones and newly found attractions to the opposite gender, we bring them all together again. Not only that, but we also bring in unsaved teens who we would never allow our children to spend time with under any other circumstances. Where did my son meet unsaved girls? Not at his Christian school or through family friends, but through our Church's Youth group.

What is the reason for putting them back together? Because we realize that, despite our attempts to evangelize and disciple these children for years, they are not there to learn about spiritual things. They are only there to socialize with one another and if we kept them separate they would not come. Or maybe, if we kept them separate, the ones who truly want to learn the things of God, and even those who are on the fence might be able to learn without distraction.

We use worldly entertainment, candy and trips to lure them in. Instead of depending on "the foolishness of preaching to save them that believe", we depend on our worldly methods. Instead of Holding up Christ, trusting in the Holy Spirit to draw them, we hold up games and prizes. These man-made ways do not save.

We even dangle our own children in front of them as bait. Then we tell these teens that they should be here to learn how to glorify God, not just for fun or to flirt with each other. We throw them all together with their raging hormones and then tell our children that they should not date the unsaved. Are we kidding?

"And one went out into the field to gather herbs, and found a wild vine, and gathered thereof wild gourds his lap full, and came and shred them into the pot of pottage: for they knew them not. So they poured out for the men to eat. And it came to pass, as they were eating of the pottage, that they cried out, and said, O thou man of God, there is death in the pot. And they could not eat thereof" (2 Kings 4:39-40).

Why would we go out and deliberately bring sin into the camp, to put a snare before our children? Why would we bring these wild vines in to mix and mingle with our children? We tell them, as well as adult Christians, over and over how that they should choose their friends wisely. We tell them to witness to the lost, and to show them Christian love and mercy, but that they should not be close friends with them. Why? Because we know that it will drag them down.

The Jews, God's chosen people, insisted that any who would be joined to them must convert to their beliefs first. Even servants were circumcised. They would not dare to bring the unsaved into the assembly of believers and call this evangelism or service to God. Evangelism and conversion must occur first. When they did mix with the unsaved, or give their daughters to be married to them, it was a sin and a reproach to the people.

Can we even begin to suggest that God would approve of such practices as allowing our children to mix and mingle with those of the unsaved? Would he bless the children of Israel for going out and bringing in the unsaved to fellowship with their children? Certainly" not!

"Which thou hast commanded by thy servants the prophets, saying, The land, unto which ye go to possess it, is an unclean land with the filthiness of the people of the lands, with their abominations, which have filled it from one end to another with their uncleanness. Now therefore give not your daughters unto their sons, neither take their daughters unto your sons, nor seek their peace or their wealth for ever: that ye may be strong, and eat the good of the land, and leave it for an inheritance to your children for ever. And after all that is come upon us for our evil deeds, and for our great trespass, seeing that thou our God hast punished us less than our iniquities deserve, and hast given us such deliverance as this; Should we again break thy commandments, and join in affinity with the people of these abominations? wouldest not thou be angry with us till thou hadst consumed us, so that there should be no remnant nor escaping?" (Ezra 9:11-14).

So, does that mean we should not evangelize teens? NO! Of course it doesn't. Please do not misunderstand. We should be doing *everything* we can to witness to these young adults and to their families, but that does not mean sacrificing the spiritual protection of our own. We must keep a biblical (and logical) perspective. We must go out and preach the gospel to them, and their families. Then those that are saved will join themselves to the Church.

Instead of making the local Church a meeting hall for the saved and unsaved alike, we should be a filling station- ministering to, exhorting and equipping believers to go out and fulfill the great commission.

We desperately need a return to biblical preaching, teaching, methods, and biblical terminology. Are we willing to embrace the truth and turn from our own ways? If what we are doing is not what God command, the way he commands, it is simply disobedience.

Will we embrace the truth, or hold to our own ways?

I know that it is difficult to hear that we have bought into a lie- that we have believed a false gospel, and turned to our own ways. It can seem overwhelming to consider the enormity of problem.

"For in much wisdom is much grief: and he that increaseth knowledge increaseth sorrow" (Ecclesiastes 1:18).

Believe me, there have been many times that I almost wished I did not see what I see, many times I would have rather not known the truth so that I could be on board with those around me. Be very careful though, because wishes like that can very easily come true.

"Take heed therefore how ye hear: for whosoever hath, to him shall be given; and whosoever hath not, from him shall be taken even that which he seemeth to have" (Luke 8:18).

I'm sure we can all think of someone we knew in the past, who at one time was a strong man or woman of God, or possibly even a well-known Preacher, who has now gone astray. One man immediately comes to my mind. He was a great Evangelist who started out with a strong biblical message of salvation, reaching many for Christ, but somehow eventually became so corrupt and ecumenical that his gospel message is no longer exclusive to Jesus Christ alone. It is now so broad and all-inclusive that even Mary worshippers are included. Is it possible that this is exactly what has happened to him?

"Therefore we ought to give the more earnest heed to the things which we have heard, lest at any time we should let them slip" (Hebrews 2:1).

I'm sure none of these men ever intended to go astray. None of them consciously decided to turn their ears from the truth, but somehow, little by little, that's what happened. What a terrible thought that we too could be headed down that same path, if we refuse to hear the truth of God's word. Don't be deceived. None of us is above being tempted. Even Fundamental Bible believers, who pride themselves on rejecting modern practices, and hold strictly to Bible doctrine can leave their first love.

"I know thy works, and thy labour, and thy patience, and how thou canst not bear them which are evil: and thou hast tried them which say they are apostles, and are not, and hast found them liars: And hast borne, and hast patience, and for my name's sake hast laboured, and hast not fainted. Nevertheless I have somewhat against thee, because thou hast left thy first love" (Revelation 2:2-4).

As a Fundamental Independent Baptist, I believe this passage can very easily be applied to us. We reject the new Bible versions and contemporary music (which we well should), and maintain biblical separation from those who preach and teach known false doctrine. We teach holiness and modesty despite the modern, worldly Christianity that surrounds us, and yet I believe we have left our first love. We have abandoned the true biblical gospel and embraced a lie. We have strained at the gnat and swallowed the camel, so to speak.

While we hold fast to our Biblical doctrines of baptism, the Lord's supper, eternal security, male preachers, ...etc., our Churches are full of unsaved, false converts! The Devil honestly couldn't be happier. As far as he's concerned, we can teach all these doctrines we want to these false converts, because he still has their souls. He's thrilled if we spend all our time trying to teach these goats how to walk and talk and act like sheep!

We can baptize them with biblical believer's baptism (if on the rare occasion our converts ever come to Church), we can insist on male leadership and even have our KJV Bible, as long as we are preaching our false gospel of "just say this prayer". Now, don't get me wrong, holding to these doctrines is of great importance, and crucial to the Church, but they can never make up for the neglecting of true gospel preaching and obedience to the Lord's commands!

> "Therefore whosoever heareth these sayings of mine, and doeth them, I will liken him unto a wise man, which built his house upon a rock: And the rain descended, and the floods came, and the winds blew, and beat upon that house; and it fell not: for it was founded upon a rock. And every one that heareth these sayings of mine, and doeth them not, shall be likened unto a foolish man, which built his house upon the sand: And the rain descended, and the floods came, and the winds blew, and beat upon that house; and it fell: and great was the fall of it" (Matthew 7:24-27).

The foundation for *all* we do must be the true gospel of Christ, not the inventions of man.

> "For other foundation can no man lay than that is laid, which is Jesus Christ. Now if any man build upon this foundation gold, silver, precious stones, wood, hay, stubble; Every man's work shall be made manifest: for the day shall declare it, because it shall be revealed by fire; and the fire shall try every man's work of what sort it is. If any man's work abide which he hath built thereupon, he shall receive a reward. If any man's work shall be burned, he shall suffer loss: but he himself shall be saved; yet so as by fire" (1 Corinthians 3:11-15).

The love of our precious Savior, Jesus and sharing the truth of his gospel, in the way that he has commanded should be what motivates us, and nothing else. Everything we do, if it is not for the love of Christ, and his word, is really only for ourselves.

Without a love of the truth, it's all just religion.

Someone with a love of the truth and a hunger for the word will constantly be seeking more of its wisdom, renewing their mind mind, "that ye may prove what is that good, and acceptable, and perfect, will of God" (Romans 12:2b).

The Bible tells us to also "Study" to show ourselves approved unto God…"

The Bereans were commended, not for their service, but for their study of the word, daily searching the scriptures to see if what they were hearing was really so. It takes time, prayer, study, and attention to the word.

They were commended for diligently comparing what they were being taught with the word of God. They would *only* accept the words of men *if* they agreed with the word of God. For them the word of God was the final authority.

"These were more noble than those in Thessalonica, in that they received the word with all readiness of mind, and searched the scriptures daily, whether those things were so" (Acts 17:11).

Today, many Christians have gotten this reversed. They compare what they are being taught, not to the word of God, but to the teachings of other men (Theologians, Evangelists, Pastors). If the plain truth of the scriptures conflicts with the teachings of men, they will choose to believe the teachings of men, allowing the words of men to be their final authority.

What is your final authority? A lack of studying and a lack of love for the word has led multitudes astray.

"Study to shew thyself approved unto God, a workman that needeth not to be ashamed, rightly dividing the word of truth" (2 Timothy 2:15)

"O how love I thy law! it is my meditation all the day. Thou through thy commandments hast made me wiser than mine enemies: for they are ever with me. I have more understanding than all my teachers: for thy testimonies are my meditation" (Psalms 119:97-99).

"More to be desired are they than gold, yea, than much fine gold: sweeter also than honey and the honeycomb" (Psalms 19:10).

"How sweet are thy words unto my taste! yea, sweeter than honey to my mouth!" (Psalms 119:103).

"For wisdom is better than rubies; and all the things that may be desired are not to be compared to it" (Proverbs 8:11).

CHAPTER 8
WE *CAN* SHARE THE GOSPEL WITHOUT MAKING FALSE CONVERTS!

If we are going to hit the mark in our children's ministries, or in any ministry for that matter, we must have the right target in sight. If we have our sights set on obtaining decisions and prayers, then that's all we will ever get. We must set our sights on biblical preaching, teaching and evangelism. Our aim should be to lead people, through the preaching of the word, to repentance toward God and faith in Jesus Christ.

In order to change our perspective on Evangelism, there is one vitally important truth that we need to really wrap our heads around and here it is: It is not our job to save them!

We are *not* commanded to *get people saved*. That is God's job.

Although we have all been duped into believing that we must go out and *get people saved*, and been rebuked for not having *led anyone to the Lord* lately; that is not the biblical command. We do not have the power to regenerate anyone upon our direction. Our job is simply to biblically educate or children, preach and teach the gospel to the lost, and then to disciple those who believe and are baptized. If we will do that; God will take care of the rest. Will we trust him?

How can we lead others to repentance and faith?

We must begin by changing our strategy and appealing to the conscience rather than merely to the will.

I remember when I was first saved, believing that we just needed to give people the answer- that Jesus paid it all! I thought that once they heard that, then of course they would be convinced to accept salvation and be changed just as I was. So, I shared the answer (the gospel) with as many as I could, and I too led those people through prayers and assured them that they were saved.

It didn't take long, however for me to see that these were empty professions from people (many children) who most often, didn't even know what the question was, or care, let alone want the answer. I could easily convince these people to say the prayers, but they were not saved, or changed. They did not become new creatures, and I had to accept that when I told them that they were saved, I had told them a lie.

Jesus *is* of course the answer, but there must be an understanding of question; and there must be a *need* for salvation.

"And when he is come, he will reprove the world of sin, and of righteousness, and of judgment" (John 16:8)

The Holy Ghost convicts the world of sin and righteousness & judgment. You can preach the gospel all day long to someone, but without conviction it will only be foolishness to them. You might even be able to convince them to accept the great offer of Heaven that you are presenting, but without a genuine understanding of their sin and condemnation before God, it is meaningless to them.

"For the preaching of the cross is to them that perish foolishness" (1 Corinthians 1:18).

Why? Because just as only they that are sick need a Physician, only they that are convicted of their sin and God's judgment upon them see their need for a Savior. Without an understanding of our condemnation before God, we cannot even see our need for a Savior. Having a fear of the Lord is the beginning of wisdom.

How does the Holy Spirit bring conviction of these things? Through the preaching of God's word, which shows God's righteous rule and reign. How can we know that we have sinned against God? Only by knowing his law can we see our offenses, and our need for a Savior. We must hold up God's undeniable standard of perfect righteousness to show how far short we all come.

It is common to hear today that we simply need to preach the death burial and resurrection of Christ so that others can put their faith in him. Often children right out of the nursery with no understanding of who God is, or his righteous judgment of their sin, or even their need for a Savior are given the gospel and instructed to simply *accept Jesus*. These children are being offered a remedy for an ailment they are not even aware that they have. There must first be conviction.

"When Jesus heard it, he saith unto them, They that are whole have no need of the physician, but they that are sick" (Mark 2:17a).

Without a knowledge of what sin is, there can be no conviction and no repentance. Through the law of God, we learn what sin is.

"… Nay, I had not known sin, but by the law: for I had not known lust, except the law had said, Thou shalt not covet" (Romans 7:7).

That is why teaching children God's laws should be a great priority for teachers and for parents. It is foundational for their Christian education. It amazes me how many young people I meet today who do not even know what the ten commandments are. Most of the older generation were raised on them, but with the push to get God out of schools and public places, the Devil has successfully hidden these important truths from our young people. While it's easy for children to see when they have displeased Mom and Dad; for them to come to a knowledge of good and evil and understand that they have sinned against our holy God, they must know his laws.

"Wherefore the law was our schoolmaster to bring us unto Christ, that we might be justified by faith" (Galatians 3:24).

Many would argue that we are no longer under the law.

"… for ye are not under the law, but under grace." (Romans 6:14)

While it is true that we are not under the law but under grace; that only applies to those who have already been saved, who have been freed from the law through faith in Christ and are no longer under its condemnation.

"But now we are delivered from the law, that being dead wherein we were held; that we should serve in newness of spirit, and not in the oldness of the letter" (Romans 7:6).

Those who have not believed are yet condemned by the law.

"For as many as have sinned without law shall also perish without law: and as many as have sinned in the law shall be judged by the law; (For not the hearers of the law are just before God, but the doers of the law shall be justified. For when the Gentiles, which have not the law, do by nature the things contained in the law, these, having not the law, are a law unto themselves: Which shew the work of the law written in their hearts, their conscience also bearing witness, and their thoughts the mean while accusing or else excusing one another;)" (Romans 2:12-15)

Using the law lawfully

"But we know that the law is good, if a man use it lawfully" (1 Timothy 1:8).

No matter how the world's standards might change, God's word never changes. It "is quick, and powerful, and sharper than any two-edged sword, piercing even to the dividing asunder of soul and spirit, and of the joints and marrow, and is a discerner of the thoughts and intents of the heart." (Hebrews 4:12)

An unsaved sinner can split hairs and argue gray areas until they're blue in the face, but God's moral standard cuts to the heart. His unchanging standard of right and wrong can convict and humble even the hardest sinner.

> "The law of the LORD is perfect, converting the soul" (Psalms 19:7).

Almost every form of Christianity shares in its acceptance of God's moral laws, making them an easy bridge for Evangelism. Most people have heard of them, even if they cannot name them all. While they can be easily offended by denominational barriers and questions of doctrine, they are generally willing to discuss the commandments.

It is a simple thing to ask someone if they are familiar with the ten commandments, explaining that they represent God's perfect standard of righteousness and asking if they would mind going through a couple to see how they are doing according to God's standard. Most people are quite happy to impress you with how *good* they believe they are.

Many who initially claim to be confident of their own righteousness, however are brought to see their sinfulness after looking at just a few. If they are honest and sincere in their self-examination, they may even see that they have broken most of God's laws.

> "For whosoever shall keep the whole law, and yet offend in one point, he is guilty of all" (James 2:10).

The law shows us our condition as lost sinners separated from God, in need of repentance and reconciliation. "Now we know that what things soever the law saith, it saith to them who are under the law: that every mouth may be stopped, and all the world may become guilty before God." (Romans 3:19)

Pointing out the condemnation of sin and the seriousness of it in God's eyes is often a surprising reality. Many will admit to lying, but don't realize how serious of an offense it is until they are confronted with the truth of scripture.

"But the fearful, and unbelieving, and the abominable, and murderers, and whoremongers, and sorcerers, and idolaters, and **all liars**, shall have their part in the lake which burneth with fire and brimstone: which is the second death" (Revelation 21:8 emphasis mine).

Some will also admit to having stolen something in their past and yet not even think much of it at this point in their lives. Often they believe that time has erased those sins and that they have since made themselves righteous. For them, understanding the truth of their condemnation is a very necessary step. They need to be shown the fact that there is a debt to pay for even sins of the past.

For some, the simple knowledge of their guilty standing before God is enough to bring them to repentance. The recognition of their just condemnation humbles them to the point where they are able to see their need for a Savior, bringing them to faith in Christ.

Others, confronted with their guilt, choose to remain in their sin and harden themselves against faith. For these still blinded by sin, the good news of Christ's sacrificial death and resurrection has little appeal. Without an acknowledgement of their sin against God and a desire to be reconciled tom, his offer holds little value to them.

"But if our gospel be hid, it is hid to them that are lost: In whom the god of this world hath blinded the minds of them which believe not, lest the light of the glorious gospel of Christ, who is the image of God, should shine unto them" (2 Corinthians 4:3-4).

They may gladly receive your offer of Heaven if it comes at no cost, or merely the cost of a prayer, but the need of genuine salvation in Christ cannot be realized apart from repentance. For this reason, we must keep taking them back to the law.

"…Wherefore he saith, God resisteth the proud, but giveth grace unto the humble" (James 4:6).

There was a lady once who had visited our Church a couple of times. One day she came forward at the invitation, bawling her eyes out. She was the very *picture* of brokenness and repentance. (Obviously, not all who are under conviction will be so visibly stirred. Most are not as emotional.)

When I took her into one of the back rooms to counsel her, I asked why she had come forward. She told me that she wanted to get saved. And very openly discussed the conviction she was under. She revealed that she was living in sin and was greatly convicted. She wanted to know what she

107

should do. I told her that if God was convicting her, and she knew that she was in sin, she should be obedient to God and turn from that sin somehow.

Sadly, that was not something she was willing to do. It seemed she wanted relief from the condemnation of her sin, but did not desire to turn from it. She definitely had Holy Spirit conviction, but there must also be a repentant heart.

"Salvation is far from the wicked: for they seek not thy statutes" (Psalms 119:155).

I could not lead her to believe that she could continue in her sin, and simply pray a prayer to make it all ok. To pronounce her saved merely because she expressed conviction of sin (without even a desire to turn from it), would have been foolish. I counseled her to be obedient to God and to continue seeking to hear his word, but I did not attempt to soothe her conviction, or lead her to believe that she was saved.

I reminded her of the clear gospel presentation she had heard during the service and made sure she understood that salvation is by grace through faith and not of works. I urged her to turn to God and be reconciled to him through faith in Christ, and also let her know that I was available to talk anytime, if she needed further counsel.

She left that day, not with an assurance of salvation, but with the knowledge of God's rightful condemnation of her sin, and well aware of the remedy for it.

I know many would disagree with me for *blowing* such a great opportunity to *get someone saved*. They would suggest that I should have simply *gotten her saved* and then worried about her sin and repentance later.

There are many reasons that people come forward and claim to want salvation, many even with tears such as this dear lady. I believe that she sincerely desired relief from her conviction, but it would have been a great disservice to her to do that. I cannot forgive her sin, or excuse it. None of us can. We do not have the power or the authority. All I could do was agree with God that her sin was indeed sin and needed to be turned from.

Although her sorrow did appear to be sincere, and it saddened me to see her leave feeling no better, I had no way of knowing whether it was godly sorrow or worldly sorrow. The only way we can even have any indication, is to see what comes from it.

"For godly sorrow worketh repentance to salvation not to be repented of: but the sorrow of the world worketh death" (2 Corinthians 7:10).

As far as I know, her circumstances have not changed. She continues to live in sin and continues to be unsaved. The last I heard, she was not attending Church anywhere regularly.

This in itself leads me to believe that her sorrow was not godly sorrow, but worldly sorrow. "Godly sorrow worketh repentance unto salvation…" (2 Corinthians 7:10) which was clearly not the case here. Her sorrow did not lead to repentance and salvation, but to a continuance in sin and destruction. Her path leads to only death; yet with a knowledge that she is still unsaved, there is hope!

She left there, not with a soothed conscience, but with a heavy load of conviction still upon her shoulders. Most importantly though, she left with the knowledge of how to be saved when she is ready to be reconciled to God.

I could have easily created a false convert that day by leading her through a prayer and assuring her of salvation, but chose to let her walk away instead, as I believe Christ himself would have done. We see an example of this in the story of the rich young ruler.

"And when he was gone forth into the way, there came one running, and kneeled to him, and asked him, Good Master, what shall I do that I may inherit eternal life? And Jesus said unto him, Why callest thou me good? there is none good but one, that is, God. Thou knowest the commandments, Do not commit adultery, Do not kill, Do not steal, Do not bear false witness, Defraud not, Honour thy father and mother. And he answered and said unto him, Master, all these have I observed from my youth. Then Jesus beholding him loved him, and said unto him, One thing thou lackest: go thy way, sell whatsoever thou hast, and give to the poor, and thou shalt have treasure in heaven: and come, take up the cross, and follow me. And he was sad at that saying, and went away grieved: for he had great possessions" (Mark 10:17-22).

This ruler came, not with tears, but with self-righteousness. He was confident that he was already prepared to received eternal life. Jesus, however demanded from him, the same thing- repentance of his sin. Jesus called him to sell all of his possessions and give them to the poor. His choice reveals how far short he had actually come from keeping all of the commandments he claimed to have kept. He went away sorrowful because he chose to love his riches more than God and himself more than others. This man was no more interested in turning from his sin that the lady I spoke with, and so went away, not will an assurance of salvation, but grieved with the knowledge of his own conviction.

Whatever reasons others might come up with, I'll choose to follow Jesus and his example instead. He knows far better how to deal with men's hearts than we do.

How did Jesus deal with those who were unrepentant or self-righteous? Jesus did not offer an easy way out to the rich young ruler, and we must resist the urge to do so ourselves. Did he ever just ignore sin and welcome them into salvation? No. He always addressed sin and the need for repentance.

We need to do the same. We must be patient enough to help prepare the soil of their hearts. Sometimes we are so eager to give others the good news that we neglect to do so. As soon as any show the slightest conviction- we rush to remove that for them and to offer them assurance. Jesus told us himself that he came to call sinners to repentance. Again, the proper order is to repent and then believe.

I am not suggesting in any way that we discourage people from making decisions to turn to God, or that we suggest that they wait, or that repentance is a lengthy process. For some it's instantaneous. But, for those who are not repentant, offering an assurance of salvation can cause permanent harm. Why would they ever repent if they believe they are forgiven already? Why would they continue seeking a cure for their disease if we convince them they are already cured? It is like telling them that they are healthy and have nothing to worry about when they are in fact, dying. The law is our schoolmaster. We need to allow it to do its work.

That does not mean we withhold the good news of salvation in Christ. Just as with the lady who came forward in tears, it is important to make them aware of the gospel, but that gospel must include repentance.

Repentant or not, we should never lead someone through a prayer and offer assurances of salvation, because we can never know who is truly saved. As we saw in Chapter 3, a prayer is neither the means nor the guarantee of salvation. Those who are repentant and express belief in the Savior should be directed to join themselves to a bible-believing Church where they should be baptized as a testimony of that belief and discipled.

They should also be directed to the scriptures to *examine themselves* and to work out their own salvation with fear and trembling, for assurance. (We will discuss assurance of salvation in much more detail in the following chapter.)

Avoiding rabbit trails.

Often, those who are dodging conviction will do everything they can to throw the light off themselves. They will very quickly attempt to divert your attention away from spiritual topics. At the very mention of God's law, they suddenly become magicians, pulling rabbits out of their hats, and hankies out of their pockets. Their dogs, their illnesses, or even their deprived childhoods, become smokescreens from which to hide behind.

The fact is, they simply don't want to deal with their conviction of sin, but most are too nice to simply chase you off. So, they attempt to distract you with their much-speaking.

While it is always important to be kind and compassionate, remember the goal. Offer to pray for their illnesses and woes, but try not to allow these to take priority over the matter of their souls.

Keep taking them back to the law. How they respond to the law will help you to gauge their conviction. If they will not acknowledge conviction, but argue against it and attempt to minimize it, then that is a pretty clear indication that they are not repentant toward God. That means the law has not yet done its work and stopped their mouth so that they are guilty before God. Until they are guilty, there can be no repentance. Remember, without repentance there can be no salvation.

"Now we know that what things soever the law saith, it saith to them who are under the law: that every mouth may be stopped, and all the world may become guilty before God" (Romans 3:19).

Some people do have sincere questions and need to be patiently instructed, answering their concerns according to scripture and helping to remove stumbling blocks. Others have no interest in spiritual things. It's important to be able to recognize the difference. Scorners and skeptics will gladly waste your time with a feigned interest in God, while attempting to disprove him to you and any others within earshot. They will take you on every rabbit trail imaginable and ask every illogical, and irrelevant question they can come up with simply as an attempt to confuse you. These questions are rarely sincere and even answering them will not lead to their enlightenment or belief, but simply to more questions. If they can stump you with their questions, they have in their own minds justified their unbelief.

"But foolish and unlearned questions avoid, knowing that they do gender strifes" (2 Timothy 2:23).

Atheists and Agnostics often make a sport of it. They will flatter you with a false interest in your Bible knowledge. This is most often meant to mock you, not to learn from you. It's important to understand this.

"A fool hath no delight in understanding, but that his heart may discover itself"(Proverbs 18:2).

According to the Bible, Atheists are fools whose only desire is to promote their foolishness. This is what God has to say about dealing with fools:

"Speak not in the ears of a fool: for he will despise the wisdom of thy words" (Proverbs 23:9).

This may seem harsh and unloving, but God knows far better than we do how they should be handled. He knows that it is a great waste of time to argue with a fool, because it is not a lack of knowledge that causes unbelief, but the willful rejection of the knowledge of God.

"The heavens declare the glory of God; and the firmament sheweth his handywork. Day unto day uttereth speech, and night unto night sheweth knowledge. There is no speech nor language, where their voice is not heard" (Psalms 19:1).

God has not called us prove his existence to Atheists or to anyone else. He has already done that.

"Because that which may be known of God is manifest in them; for God hath shewed it unto them. For the invisible things of him from the creation of the world are clearly seen, being understood by the things that are made, even his eternal power and Godhead; so that they are without excuse: Because that, when they knew God, they glorified him not as God, neither were thankful; but became vain in their imaginations, and their foolish heart was darkened. Professing themselves to be wise, they became fools" (Romans 1:19-22).

The reason they reject the knowledge of God is simple. They do not want to submit to his authority. God has called us to share the gospel- the reason for the hope that is within us. We are to be making disciples through spreading the gospel. If they will not believe in God, then they cannot receive the gospel and be reconciled to God.

"But without faith it is impossible to please him: for he that cometh to God must believe that he is, and that he is a rewarder of them that diligently seek him" (Hebrews 11:6).

We need to be obedient to God's word and not lean to our own understanding. When they will not believe in God, we must brush the dust off our feet and keep going. We cannot allow them to keep us from our commission. There are some out there with repentant hearts ready to receive the good news! Many times, we want so badly for people to see the truth that we chase these rabbit trails far beyond what is profitable. As a matter of fact, most often we do more harm than good when we engage them. Doing this in front of others can become even more disastrous.

> "Answer not a fool according to his folly, lest thou also be like unto him (Proverbs 26:4).

Often, instead of answering their baited questions, I will ask, "Even if you could prove that God is unfair, or unloving, or whatever other accusations you might have against him; would that prove that he does not exist? (Most will concede that it would not, because no one can prove that God does not exist.) No matter what you think of God, and his character, he is still God and you will one day stand before him. So, whether you believe he is unfair, or unloving, he will still judge you. You can agree with him now and get on board with his plan, or you can disagree with him all the way to Hell. It's your choice, but it is not *his* desire that you go to Hell."

Now I'll admit that to my knowledge, no one has ever repented and come to Christ because of that, but it does generally cut off the argument and hopefully leave them with something to think about.

As soon as we accept the challenge to answer all their loaded questions, it becomes a war of words, so to speak. We in essence, draw a line in the sand- us against their intentionally pointed arguments. At that point, they cease to cooperate with us in a desire to seek the truth, but now steel themselves to win this intellectual battle at all costs.

Jehovah's witnesses are masters at this. They will ask questions specifically geared at destroying your beliefs. Often, they will patiently listen as you offer explanations, allowing you to feel as though you are helping them to understand. They may even ask if they can come back and talk again. This is how many Christians are deceived into allowing them into their homes. The Jehovah's witnesses will then continue to ask question after question until they finally get you to one you cannot answer. That is when their true motives surface.

While they have been allowing you to think you are showing them the truth, they have actually been planting seeds of doubt and deception in your mind. When they see that they have successfully gotten you to where you can no longer answer their questions; it is then that they show you the answer. Therefore, God's word tells us:

> "If there come any unto you, and bring not this doctrine, receive him not into your house, neither bid him God speed: For he that biddeth him God speed is partaker of his evil deeds (2 John 1:10-11).

If someone comes to you with a false gospel message, you can be sure their only goal is to give you that message, not to learn from you. If they did not firmly believe what they were promoting, they would not be doing it. They are on a mission. No matter how they might fool you, you are not teaching them! That is why God tells us not to receive them into our houses or even to wish them a good day. Their mission is only evil. No matter how much Bible you know, don't kid yourself; you are not above being fooled.

Dealing with children presents even more challenges.

Because we know that a child's intellect is limited, often we are tempted to oversimplify the gospel message and use our own man-made terminology instead. We must resist the urge to downplay the truth of the gospel. We as Bible believers claim to hold every word of God in high regard, and yet we have replaced God's perfect word with our own inaccurate and often misleading catch phrases.

If a child is too immature to understand the concepts of repentance and faith, then we *must* accept that they are probably too young to be saved. That does not mean that we abandon any effort to teach them. It simply means that we cannot expect to harvest what is not ready. We can however, sow the seed, water and then trust God for the increase.

God's word can do even what we cannot. We must keep in mind that the word of God is spiritual it speaks to the heart, not merely the intellect. It is spirit and it is life. It's quick and powerful and sharper than a two-edged sword. It can speak to hearts, and bring conviction and faith if we will plant the true seed of the word. This takes time. We need to be patient when dealing with children and allow the word to do its work within their hearts. We must put aside our foolish desires for instant results and commit to however long it takes.

We know that children do not learn every life lesson we teach them the very first time. How much more difficult must it be for them to really learn the spiritual? I remember when my children were small, teaching them to look both ways before we crossed the street. We practiced over and over and repeated the rules every time. They could recite them frontwards and backwards, and yet, the first time they had the opportunity to chase a ball into the street, they each did so without looking. They knew what the right thing to do was, but it had not yet become something that they could apply for themselves.

Often, we view their spiritual teaching as something that is much the same, merely facts that they can recite, which have not yet been tested. Because they repeat the right answers back to us and seem to know the correct meaning, we assume that what we are teaching has already accomplished the necessary work within their hearts.

Superficial Bible teaching is not enough. Many of our children grow up hearing Bible stories, but without a solid understanding of doctrine and the ability to properly apply them, they are just stories. Even with teaching the correct doctrine and application and earnestly conveying the spiritual principles intended, we cannot know if the child has properly understood them until the time that they are called upon to use them.

We must keep teaching and guiding them and reminding them over and over until it finally shows forth in their lives. This is the greatest problem with our easy Believeism mentality. We think that because they said a prayer at whatever young age, that they have understood and believed, therefore we can simply encourage them and teach them how to live like Christians and they will be fine.

They are not fine! The majority have never even truly been saved. Most have never even seen themselves as hopeless sinners in need of salvation because we gave them a false salvation before they ever knew what sin was. Coming to repentance isn't even a consideration for them because they already *asked Jesus into their hearts*. We have completely dropped the ball in their Christian education.

Our children are bombarded daily from every possible angle, everywhere they go. They are being *educated* every minute of every day through the TV, radio, internet, the market place, influences of liberal Christianity and unsaved family members, and worst of all, through public education. Yet, we think that if we tell them a couple of stories, play some games and lead them through a prayer that they will stand firm in the faith? Are we kidding?

We are failing them on the very highest level. When they go off to college, they are attacked by Liberals and Evolutionists who are well-armed and prepared to destroy their faith. Yet, we have failed to teach our children solid doctrine, or even creation. They are often unarmed, completely vulnerable, and made to feel foolish for their lack of knowledge. They are unable to give answer for the reason of the hope that is within them. We need to take their Christian education much, much more seriously.

Years ago, as a new Christian, I worked in a flower shop owned by a Muslim family. I was so excited to share with them the truth of salvation through Jesus Christ (I had taken a short Sunday school course about dealing with false religions and was confident that I was prepared to answer their false teachings). Little did I know that I was almost completely ignorant of the amount of teaching they themselves had received.

I bragged of how we had Bible clubs every Wednesday night for all the kids. I told them how we played games and had snacks and shared a Bible story each week, with our goal being to teach them a Bible verse.

How foolish I felt when I heard how they educated their own children. I was told how they brought their children together *every* evening, and taught them, not *verses* of the Koran, but *chapters*, and get this- *without* snacks and games. Why? Because they take their religion very seriously. Now, that is not to hold them up as a positive example for belief, because obviously, Islam is false; but why should false religions such this, or Jehovah's witnesses or Mormons be so zealous while we are so lax?

If this false religion that has not the indwelling Holy Spirit of God can be this diligent in teaching their children the beliefs that they claim, what excuse can we possibly have for doing so much less?

CHAPTER 9
ASSURANCE OF SALVATION

Recently, a young woman asked me if *she* was saved. I gave her the only honest, biblical answer I knew. I said, "I don't know."

Although this young woman had made a profession of faith and showed some interest in the things of God, I would never assure her or anyone else that they are saved because the Bible tells us that only God can see her heart. We merely observe the fruits (evidences), or the lack thereof. We cannot know with certainty anyone else's salvation.

The Bible tells us that many "profess that they know God; but in works they deny him..." (Titus 1:16).

Many, it says, will say "lord, Lord..." and spend an eternity in Hell because they were NOT truly saved. Woe to me if I help send them there with a false assurance!

Only she and God can ever truly know if her salvation is genuine. That's why the Bible tells us to "work out your own salvation with fear and trembling (Philippians 2:12), and to Examine yourselves, whether ye be in the faith; prove your own selves (2 Corinthians 13:5).

This question of the assurance of salvation is something that many of our converts struggle with. In my years as a Christian I have heard (and to my shame, even offered) many different answers, some biblical, but most were not even close. Often, we rely on experiences, philosophies, or traditions to answer that question for us.

-Did you *say a prayer* or *ask Jesus into your heart*?
-Did you *really mean it* when you *decided* to be saved?
-Did you believe the facts of salvation?
-Did you make a commitment?

Notice how the emphasis is always on what the professing believer has done instead of what God should have done in their hearts? Notice too that none of these *proofs* can be found in scripture.

Most soul-winning programs emphasize giving converts an assurance of salvation immediately upon profession. I have heard it explained that there's nothing sadder than someone who cannot rest in their salvation but continually questions it. So, we are instructed to show them verses that (supposedly) prove their salvation, as well as the eternal security of it.

While the issue of eternal security- the matter of not losing your salvation is one that certainly needs to be taught, often the heart of the problem for these questioning converts is the *genuineness* of their salvation.

Many who were promised salvation without repentance, based merely on a prayer, eventually become so burdened with their own sin that they fear to have *lost* what they never truly had. The reason we have to work so hard to convince them of their eternal security is probably because we *got them saved* by our Decisional regeneration/Easy Believeism gospel.

If we lead people to believe that they are magically saved by a decision, and a prayer. Is it really any wonder that they doubt the security of their salvation? If they believe that they merely decided and prayed, then certainly it would make sense that they could *un-decide*. When we begin to teach the truth of salvation, starting with repentance toward God and faith in Christ, and about regeneration evidenced by the workings of the Holy Spirit, it will be much easier then to teach them the eternal security of their salvation.

I listened to a sermon once about how most professing Christians today are actually still lost. It talked about their sinful lifestyles and lack of fruit being evidence of their unregenerate state *despite* their professions. It accurately described the difficulty in reaching those who believe that they are already saved.

The message was very good and clearly spelled out a great problem within the Church today. The glaringly obvious question however, would have to be: Why do all of these people think they are saved in the first place? Ummm... Do you think maybe it's because *we not only told them, but also assured them that they are?*

Our faulty evangelism techniques are causing the problem! Why would we assure anyone that they are saved simply because we coerced them into praying a prayer? Did it ever occur to us that telling people who may not be saved that they are, may be sending them to Hell? -While telling someone who *is* saved that they may not be can do them no spiritual harm at all?

Why would we make such efforts to convince someone that they can trust their souls to a mere profession when the Bible does not say that? The Bible warns over and over of those who are deceived and admonishes believers to "Examine yourselves, whether ye be in the faith; prove your own selves" (2 Corinthians 13:5).

"Not every one that saith unto me, Lord, Lord, shall enter into the kingdom of heaven; but he that doeth the will of my Father which is in heaven. Many will say to me in that day, Lord, Lord, have we not prophesied in thy name? and in thy name have cast out devils? and in thy name done many wonderful works? And then will I profess unto them, I never knew you: depart from me, ye that work iniquity" (Matthew 7:21-23).

The Lord tells us that there will be many who will stand before him and say…"Lord, Lord…" These are people who honestly believed they were saved from the punishment of their sins; but in fact, that condemnation remained. Why would they be so deceived? Why would they be so sure of something that is not true? What would convince them of such a lie?

> "Because with lies ye have made the heart of the righteous sad, whom I have not made sad; and strengthened the hands of the wicked, that he should not return from his wicked way, by promising him life" (Ezekiel 13:22).

These were *saved* by saying a prayer and were told that if they simply prayed to asked Jesus into their heart, then they could rest assured that they are indeed saved. They were also told that if they ever doubt their salvation, they can look back to the day they said that prayer and know that they are saved.

I must say that if they must look back at a prayer for assurance, it can only mean that nothing else has changed enough to convince them. There must be no change of life or change of mind- no fruit or other evidence of the indwelling Holy Spirit of Christ. It must mean that they have not really become a new creature, or been brought to newness of life.

If that moment of profession is all they have to hold onto then what an empty, meaningless salvation they must have. Where is the abundant life? Or fullness of joy? Where is the peace of God which passes all understanding? If the only thing they have to show for their salvation is a prayer from a desperately wicked heart that is deceitful beyond measure, no wonder so many doubt their salvation in Christ. They should! Obviously, they have only been "saved" by a prayer; because if they had been saved by Christ, they would know it. How sad that so many have been deceived.

When I was in my late twenties, I was led through a sinner's prayer and told that if I really meant it, that I was now saved. Well, I certainly did mean it, just as much as I meant the Our Father's and Hail Mary's I said every night! Of course I meant it; but I was not saved. My heart was not changed, and neither were my desires. I continued to live in sin for quite a few years after that.

I would occasionally tell people I was a born-again Christian, but I honestly had no idea what that meant. I often doubted the truth of my salvation. Many years later, the Lord led me to repentance and faith, and I was truly born again. At that point, everything changed- my heart, my desires and my life. When true salvation came, I NEVER doubted my salvation again. How could I? The presence of the Holy Spirit of Christ within me has been a constant and undeniable evidence.

Any time someone questions their salvation, instead of allowing the Holy Spirit of God to convict them or show them their true state we rush to offer them something to push that doubt aside. We offer excuses for those who may have never repented or experienced any real change in their lives. We suggest that they are merely carnal or at least struggling against sin and quickly point out that even David, a man after God's own heart, sinned. I'm sure David would turn over in his grave if he knew how many sins were reasoned away in his name.

This was the case with a man I knew of once who professed salvation and got baptized. Although he attended Church and even served there, he also continued in adultery, immorality, drunkenness, anger, cursing and blasphemy for twenty years. It appeared that the only thing that had really changed in his life was the fact that he now attended and participated in Church. When he went to his Pastor questioning his salvation, the Pastor assured him that as long as he believed the facts of Jesus' death, burial, and resurrection that he was surely saved.

Now, did *I know* that that man was *not* saved? Of course not. I could not see his heart. All I could see were the evidences. Did his Pastor *know* that he *was* saved? No! All he had to go by were the visible evidences as well (which overwhelmingly pointed to the contrary). Why are we so anxious to assure people of what we do not *know* ourselves?

A woman I know of also went to her Pastor for counsel when she began to believe that her salvation experience may have been false. She was looking at her life of immorality and experiencing great conviction that she never had before. Again, her Pastor assured her that she was indeed saved. She eventually came to genuine salvation and was born again. She *knows* now without a doubt that she was not saved when she was originally led to believe that she was.

Why is it that we are so anxious to offer assurances to others to soothe over any conviction or discomfort as quickly as possible? We offer them a reminder of the prayer they said, or the commitment they felt, or even belief in the facts of salvation; but did we ever stop to think that these doubts were from God, to warn them of deception? Maybe he wants them to question and turn to Him for the answer. After all, only *he* knows their hearts. Instead, we want to tell them it's the Devil wanting them to doubt. Why would the Devil want them to doubt their salvation? Wouldn't it suit his purposes more to have them deceived by a false salvation?

What if we are quenching what might very well be Holy Spirit conviction? What if we are the reason that someone stands before the Lord and hears, "I never knew you: depart from me, ye that work iniquity" (Matthew 7:23)

> "Then said he unto the disciples, It is impossible but that offences will come: but woe unto him, through whom they come!" (Luke 17:1).

Many will *profess* to believe in Christ, but in the end Christ will *profess* that He does not know them. For those people, their professions are worthless. Don't let them be deceived because of us. It is not our job to seal the deal or to give assurances. That job belongs to the Holy Spirit. We are only to preach the gospel, then baptize and teach those who believe. Nowhere does the Bible say that we seal the deal with a prayer and pronounce them saved. We need to stop making excuses for what we are doing- calling them back-sliders and carnal Christians, and change the way we evangelize. We need to get back to Bible truths and put aside these man-made traditions.

Trying to assure someone else of salvation is presumptuous and unbiblical. Holding up the holy word of God, on the other hand, is good and profitable for all. We cannot know who truly has saving faith and who doesn't, until we see the fruits of their salvation which result in a changed life, and even then, we can never be sure they are saved. Only God and they themselves can know for sure.

A man's actions, or outward appearance can be a pretty good indication of his heart condition, but we can never really know someone else's heart. The Bible tells us that we cannot even know our own hearts, because we are deceived by them.

"The heart is deceitful above all things, and desperately wicked: who can know it?" (Jeremiah 17:9).

It is only by God's law that we see our own sinfulness and can recognize our true heart condition before God. We would never believe that our hearts were wicked or rebellious, because someone told us they were.

"... I had not known sin, but by the law: for I had not known lust, except the law had said, Thou shalt not covet" (Romans 7:7).

We need to stop telling people that they are saved and let them tell us- with their mouths and with their lives! Are they testifying to their salvation through baptism, Church attendance or a changed life? Our job is merely to preach the gospel and tell them how to be saved. We must trust God for the rest. We are never told to pronounce them saved (especially falsely).

Why is it that we do not simply point them to scripture for their assurance? Over and over again we see verses and passages that describe new life and fruits of salvation as well as the evidences of deception for the false convert. If we truly believe that God's word is truth, shouldn't we simply point them to his word? There they would find either comfort and assurance or necessary conviction.

Why does God tell us to examine ourselves? Because when he assures us that we are truly saved, we will know it, and no one will be able to convince us otherwise. It is not our place to give assurance to anyone. Only God can give true assurance. Only by the presence of the regenerating Holy Spirit of God within us can anyone be sure.

Offering a child an assurance of salvation is even more dangerous.

Because children are so trusting and excitable, we can easily mistake their enthusiasm for true faith. We must be realistic in dealing with them, knowing that they are easily deceived and immature in their understanding.

"That we henceforth be no more children, tossed to and fro, and carried about with every wind of doctrine, by the sleight of men, and cunning craftiness, whereby they lie in wait to deceive" (Ephesians 4:14).

Children very often claim to understand things which in truth are beyond their comprehension. They lack the ability to make wise or lasting decisions.

"Foolishness is bound in the heart of a child…" (Proverbs 22:15).

Their eagerness to please alone, makes them especially vulnerable to manipulation. Group evangelism, is probably the least effective and most damaging of all of our methods.

Think about it… How many times do we ask a child or adult to signify by the raised hand or other means, that they are saved? Every time we do this, we are re-enforcing the lie to those who are not truly saved. This doesn't even take into account the obvious element of peer pressure which inevitably effects their decision as well. If they are not saved, then every time we assure them, we may be leading them further from salvation. The more often a lie is repeated, the more it is believed. Practice makes permanent.

Often, parents or teachers are so convinced of the child's salvation, that they feel the need to keep assuring that child, when they doubt. We must resist the urge to assure what we cannot know. Parents and teachers should be just as actively seeking to guard these children from false assurances.

Children's hearts are also very fickle. What they desired one day may be furthest from their thoughts the next. Only when these professed convictions are lived up to without compulsion can we even be convinced that they are sincere. Many children run from God as soon as they are in a position to make decisions for themselves.

They lack the foresight to understand the consequences of their actions.

This is evidenced by their fearlessness. They have not yet exercised their own decision making enough to have experienced the consequences. Only when we see the genuine fruits emerging from their lives can we have any indication at all of someone else's regeneration. It is the job of the Holy Spirit to assure, not the parent or teacher, or even the soul-winner. Only biblical evidences should be used to judge the genuineness of regeneration-not feelings or decisions; and even then, we can never be sure and should not offer our assurances.

While we protect them from false assurances, we must also be careful to avoid dismissing their interest because of their immaturity. All spiritual interest should be cultivated and used to further their instruction. We should encourage children to *choose this day whom they will serve,* and heartily confirm their decision; but we must keep in mind that it cannot be viewed as *proof* of true salvation. Our aim should be to help them follow God, so that one day they will understand their need of salvation.

Biblical Evidences of Salvation

The very first test we can examine ourselves with is: have we been obedient in believer's baptism? This is the very first commandment given to those who profess faith.

"He that saith, I know him, and keepeth not his commandments, is a liar, and the truth is not in him" (1 John 2:4).

While baptism is not a proof and does not save; it *is an evidence,* usually the first public testimony that a believer is associating himself with Jesus Christ and taking on the name of Christ. There are of course times that new believers are physically unable to be baptized, (such as illness or imprisonment). This does not in any way prevent them from being saved.

Baptism is a command given to believers and is a very serious matter. Because of our Easy Believeism, we tend to neglect adult baptism and accept instead, a sinner's prayer as the public testimony; but when it comes to children, we seem to be overly eager to baptize them. Why? Obviously, it's more difficult to convince an adult to be baptized and publicly testify to the faith he claims. This alone should be a red flag. Baptism is a very important thing for believers and not to be neglected or minimized in its importance.

Being baptized is a public testimony not only of conversion, but also of a conscious decision to associate one's life with Christ. This clearly implies that the believer is in possession of his own life and in control of his own decisions. Obviously, adults are assumed to be responsible for making their own decisions and capable of standing in public profession of their salvation. Even they can choose to be baptized for the wrong reasons-some for penance, or religion, others just to satisfy the expectations of others.

Many adults associate their baptism with salvation and convince themselves of salvation when it may not be real. How much easier is it for a child to be deceived by such an act?

We need to be especially careful how we handle this with children. If an adult claims to believe and desires to be baptized, we assume that he has been born again and is desiring to profess that and publicly associate his life with Christ. If his testimony proves to be false, then (provided we have not been the ones to offer him a false assurance) the sincerity of his profession and commitment to live as a Christian is his own to judge.

If a child is not truly saved at the point of his baptism then becomes saved later as an adult, then their baptism was not biblical and would need to be performed again upon true salvation. Many claim this new birth as merely a recommitment, not willing to admit that their previous profession was not backed up by genuine regeneration. They are then in disobedience to the ordinance of believer's baptism. Could we be the reason they are in disobedience to the ordinance of baptism? If we make the decision that they are ready to be baptized before they are actually showing themselves ready to answer for themselves, we may be.

For this reason, it should be considered very carefully whether a child should be allowed to be baptized before that child has begun to assume responsibility for his own life decisions. How will we know? Trust me, when they begin to make their own decisions on how they will live, it's easy to see. Most children begin stepping out from under their parents' authority long before they leave home.

A parent who allows a child who has not yet exercised his own control regarding life decisions, to be baptized may be feeding into a false assurance and robbing the child of a very important experience. When that child, who may not have been saved at the time of his childhood baptism assumes responsibility for his life and turns the other direction instead; the memory of his baptism may in itself be a false assurance of salvation.

How can anyone have biblical assurance that they are truly in the faith?

"Hereby know we that we dwell in him, and he in us, because he hath given us of his Spirit" (1 John 4:13).

The Bible gives us many assurances or "proofs" to examine ourselves by.

These are related to the indwelling Holy Spirit present within every truly born-again believer.

"Now if any man have not the Spirit of Christ, he is none of his" (Romans 8:9).

"He [the Apostle Paul] said unto them, Have ye received the Holy Ghost since ye believed?" (Acts 19:2).

Instead of offering our own faulty assurances, maybe we should ask the question Paul asked, "Have you received the Holy Spirit since you believed?" If they have truly been born-again by the Holy Spirit of Christ, the Spirit *will* witness of itself.

"The Spirit itself beareth witness with our spirit, that we are the children of God" (Romans 8:16).

Here are some biblical evidences to help others test their own salvation by. These are ways in which the Holy Spirit works in our lives and witnesses of itself when we are truly saved.

1.The Holy Spirit regenerates us (brings us to new life). Could a dead man be brought to life without recognizable changes?

"Even when we were dead in sins, hath quickened us together with Christ, (by grace ye are saved;)" (Ephesians 2:5).

"Jesus answered and said unto him, Verily, verily, I say unto thee, Except a man be born again, he cannot see the kingdom of God" (John 3:3).

2. The Holy Spirit enlightens us, and brings us from darkness to light. Those who were once blind to spiritual things now see. (Could a blind man suddenly begin to see and not know it with certainty?)

"In whom the god of this world hath blinded the minds of them which believe not, lest the light of the glorious gospel of Christ, who is the image of God, should shine unto them" (2 Corinthians 4:4).

"But the natural man receiveth not the things of the Spirit of God: for they are foolishness unto him: neither can he know them, because they are spiritually discerned" (1 Corinthians 2:14).

3. The Holy Spirit gives us new desires to live pleasing to God. Instead of living to see how far we can push the rules, we begin to instead see how closely we can follow them. Our love for the Savior brings a desire to please Him.

"And hereby we do know that we know him, if we keep his commandments" (1John 2:3).

"He that saith, I know him, and keepeth not his commandments, is a liar, and the truth is not in him. But whoso keepeth his word, in him verily is the love of God perfected: hereby know we that we are in him" (1 John 2:4-5).

"Jesus answered and said unto him, If a man love me, he will keep my words" (John 14:23).

4. The Holy Spirit gives us discernment. The Holy Spirit gives us an understanding of spiritual things and helps us to recognize error.

"We are of God: he that knoweth God heareth us; he that is not of God heareth not us. Hereby know we the spirit of truth, and the spirit of error" (1 John 4:6).

"My sheep hear my voice, and I know them, and they follow me"(John 10:27)

5. The Holy Spirit gives us a love for the Brethren. Those who were once peculiar laughingstocks become the ones we desire to spend time with, and be like.

"We know that we have passed from death unto life, because we love the brethren" (1 John 3:14).

6. The Holy Spirit gives us fruits if the Spirit.

"But the fruit of the Spirit is love, joy, peace, longsuffering, gentleness, goodness, faith, Meekness, temperance: against such there is no law. And they that are Christ's have crucified the flesh with the affections and lusts" (Galatians 5:22-24).

Without the Holy Spirit's presence, often the works of the flesh are more evident:
"Now the works of the flesh are manifest, which are these; Adultery, fornication, uncleanness, lasciviousness, Idolatry, witchcraft, hatred, variance, emulations, wrath, strife, seditions, heresies, Envyings,

murders, drunkenness, revellings, and such like: of the which I tell you before, as I have also told you in time past, that they which do such things shall not inherit the kingdom of God" (Galatians 5:19-21).

"Know ye not that the unrighteous shall not inherit the kingdom of God? Be not deceived: neither fornicators, nor idolaters, nor adulterers, nor effeminate, nor abusers of themselves with mankind, Nor thieves, nor covetous, nor drunkards, nor revilers, nor extortioners, shall inherit the kingdom of God" (1 Corinthians 6:9-10).

7. The Holy Spirit gives us a desire to tell others of Christ. Could a dead man be brought to life or a blind man receive his sight and NOT want to tell others of this great and precious Savior?

"Jesus answered and said unto him, If a man love me, he will keep my words" (John 14:23).

"And he said unto them, Go ye into all the world, and preach the gospel to every creature" (Mark 16:15).

8. The Holy Spirit gives us true assurance. ONLY the Holy Spirit of Christ within us can give us a true assurance.

"Herein is our love made perfect, that we may have boldness in the day of judgment: because as he is, so are we in this world. 18 There is no fear in love; but perfect love casteth out fear: because fear hath torment. He that feareth is not made perfect in love" (1 John 4:17-18).
  If we still fear and doubt our salvation, how can we have boldness in the day of judgement?

"And hereby we know that he abideth in us, by the Spirit which he hath given us" (1 John 3:24).

We may not recognize every one of these evidences in our lives, but if we have the indwelling Spirit of Christ within us, we WILL know it.

Have YOU received the Holy Spirit since you believed? If not, it may be that you are not truly saved. Be sure. Repent and call upon the Lord today, confessing and forsaking your sin, and put your trust in Jesus. He will forgive you and cleanse you from all unrighteousness. The Holy Spirit of Christ will begin to live within you and give you eternal life. If you have repented and believed in Christ today, find a Bible-believing Church, be baptized as a testimony of your faith, and read your Bible every day.

The word of God is sufficient to both save and assure.

Let me say that again: The word of God is sufficient to both save and assure.

"...work out your OWN salvation with fear and trembling" (Philippians 2:12).

"Wherefore the rather, brethren, give diligence to make your calling and election sure: for if ye do these things, ye shall never fall" (2 Peter 1:10).

"Therefore if any man be in Christ, he is a new creature: old things are passed away; behold, all things are become new" (2 Corinthians 5:17).

"Know ye not that the unrighteous shall not inherit the kingdom of God? Be not deceived: neither fornicators, nor idolaters, nor adulterers, nor effeminate, nor abusers of themselves with mankind, Nor thieves, nor covetous, nor drunkards, nor revilers, nor extortioners, shall inherit the kingdom of God" (1 Corinthians 6:9-10).

"For this ye know, that no whoremonger, nor unclean person, nor covetous man, who is an idolater, hath any inheritance in the kingdom of Christ and of God" (Ephesians 5:5).

"They profess that they know God; but in works they deny him, being abominable, and disobedient, and unto every good work reprobate" (Titus 1:16).

"If we say that we have fellowship with him, and walk in darkness, we lie, and do not the truth" (1 John 1:6).

"He that saith, I know him, and keepeth not his commandments, is a liar, and the truth is not in him" (1 John 2:4).

"He that saith he is in the light, and hateth his brother, is in darkness even until now" (1 John 2:9).

"Love not the world, neither the things that are in the world. If any man love the world, the love of the Father is not in him.16 For all that is in the world, the lust of the flesh, and the lust of the eyes, and the pride of life, is not of the Father, but is of the world" (1 John 2:15).

"They went out from us, but they were not of us; for if they had been of us, they would no doubt have continued with us: but they went out, that they might be made manifest that they were not all of us" (1 John 2:19).

"Whosoever is born of God doth not commit sin; for his seed remaineth in him: and he cannot sin, because he is born of God. In this the children of God are manifest, and the children of the devil: whosoever doeth not righteousness is not of God, neither he that loveth not his brother" (1 John 3:9).

"And he that keepeth his commandments dwelleth in him, and he in him. And hereby we know that he abideth in us, by the Spirit which he hath given us" (1 John 3:24).

"Herein is our love made perfect, that we may have boldness in the day of judgment: because as he is, so are we in this world.18 There is no fear in love; but perfect love casteth out fear: because fear hath torment. He that feareth is not made perfect in love" (1 John 4:17).

"These things have I written unto you that believe on the name of the Son of God; that ye may know that ye have eternal life, and that ye may believe on the name of the Son of God" (1 John 5:13).

"And this is the record, that God hath given to us eternal life, and this life is in his Son. 12 He that hath the Son hath life; and he that hath not the Son of God hath not life" (1 John 5:11-12).

"But the natural man receiveth not the things of the Spirit of God: for they are foolishness unto him: neither can he know them, because they are spiritually discerned" (1 Corinthians 2:14).

ABOUT THE AUTHOR

A former false convert, Sandra M. Platt has a heart to see others come to a genuine knowledge of salvation. Since being saved, in the Spring of 1998, she has had a passion for God's word and a strong desire to help others to earnestly contend for the faith. Sandra and her husband, Jim live in Altoona, PA. and have been blessed with four children.

Bibliography

The Anxious Bench -John Williamson Nevin, Titus books New Zealand (2013)

Jamieson, Fausset & Brown, . "Commentary on Exodus 30 by Jamieson, Fausset & Brown." Blue Letter Bible. Last Modified 19 Feb, 2000. https://www.blueletterbible.org/Comm/jfb/Exd/Exd_030.cfm

Sermon Index, Revivals And Church History- Hindrances to Revival by Charles G. Finney Last Modified March 16, 2004 http://img.sermonindex.net/modules/newbb/viewtopic_pdf.php?topic_id=1549&forum=40

Strong's Greek Lexicon "G1941 - epikaleō - Strong's Greek Lexicon (KJV)." Blue Letter Bible. Accessed 5 Mar, 2017. https://www.blueletterbible.org//lang/Lexicon/Lexicon.cfm?Strongs=G1941&t=KJV

Strong's Greek Lexicon "G3341 - metanoia - Strong's Greek Lexicon (KJV)." Blue Letter Bible. Accessed 1 Mar, 2017. https://www.blueletterbible.org//lang/Lexicon/Lexicon.cfm?Strongs=G3341&t=KJV

Made in the USA
Middletown, DE
30 March 2017